Ancient
Cyprus

Veronica Tatton-Brown

Published for the Trustees of the British Museum by British Museum Press

To my parents

The Trustees of the British Museum
gratefully acknowledge
the generosity of the
A.G. Leventis Foundation.

Published by
British Museum Press
A division of
The British Museum Company Ltd
46 Bloomsbury Street
London WC1B 3QQ

First published 1987
Second edition 1997

A catalogue record for this book is
available from the British Library

ISBN 0-7141-2120-7

Designed by Martin Richards
Cover and series design by
Carroll Associates

Typeset in Van Dijck®

Manufactured in China by Imago

Cover illustration *Vase in the form of
a bull, made of Base Ring ware with
white painted decoration. From Maroni,
1400-1200 BC. Length 16 cm (6.3 in).*

This page *Ox-shaped flask (askos) of
Black-on-Red ware. From Kourion
(Curium), 750-600 BC.
Height 19 cm (7.5 in).*

Contents

Preface

Cypriot antiquities are housed in many museums in the world, but the British Museum is fortunate in possessing one of the largest collections outside Cyprus itself. This collection provides most of the illustrations for this book, which aims to tell the story of Cyprus from the beginning of its history until the end of the Roman era. The thematic treatment used here was first suggested by the Australian scholar and diplomat Dr Robert Merrillees. This revised second edition is intended to be more comprehensive than the first and is not linked to any particular exhibition. Thus the story of the British Museum's collection is not repeated here, and an additional chapter on architecture and mosaics has been added. Again the A.G. Leventis Foundation has provided generous support to help make this publication possible.

Map of the Mediterranean and the Near East.

Chapter One | The natural history of Cyprus

THE CLIMATE and vegetation of Cyprus are typically Mediterranean. The landscape is dominated by mountains, the Kyrenia range in the north and the Troodos massif in the south [1]. Between the two lies a large central plain. A typical feature is the thick hard deposit of *havara* or *kafkalla* (broadly translatable as limestone), sometimes overlying a layer of *terra rossa* (red soil) on the plateaux and ridges. There are perennial fresh water springs at Lapithos and Kythrea in the north, but apart from these there are no rivers which are free-flowing all the year round. The major rivers, with their rough stony beds, are dry in summer but flow torrentially, breaking their banks, in winter. The rainfall in antiquity may have been higher, but it is likely that as today the continuous supply of fresh water was limited and unreliable, since it would have depended on the snowfall in the Troodos and the rainfall elsewhere on the island.

Our information about the land in antiquity, before its modification by human effort, and the plant and animal life it supported comes from the analysis of pollen, botanical remains and bones from archaeological excavations, representations in art and the occasional written record. Chief among the literary sources is an anecdote recorded by Strabo in the first century AD and attributed to his fellow geographer Eratosthenes of the second century BC. He tells that authorisation was given to any inhabitant to cut down as many trees as he could and keep the cleared land as his own property tax-free. The countryside was covered by thick forests which hampered cultivation, and the activities of

1 *View of the Troodos mountains from near the monastery of Panayia Khrysorroyiatissa (Our Lady of the Golden Pomegranate).*

the timber-cutters requiring fuel for copper-smelting or ship-building timber had failed to clear enough land. The wealth of the island was legendary. 'Cyprus is second to none of the islands of the Mediterranean: it is rich in wine and oil, produces grain in abundance and possesses extensive copper mines at Tamassos', wrote Strabo in AD 23.

The lowlands, comprising the central plain and the strip of land around the coast, were made up of marshlands and rich fertile meadows. Many weeds grow in these areas today and several of these species have been identified in Late Bronze Age contexts. Seed remains show that wheat and barley were cultivated by early settlers, and gold beads in the shape of grains of wheat form parts of necklaces of the later second millennium. Date palms and poppies were also grown by the early inhabitants. The date palm in part inspired representations of the 'tree of life' and the palmette, and palm trees are also among the motifs decorating

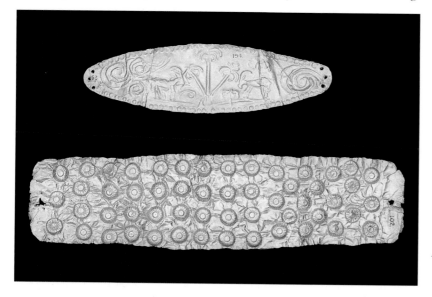

2 Gold mouthpiece and diadem made in Cyprus in the Late Bronze Age. Both are funerary: the former originally covered the mouth and the latter was placed on the skull of a skeleton. The mouthpiece, from Enkomi, is decorated with goats and palm trees and the diadem with small rosettes. Length of diadem 20.8 cm (8.2 in).

funerary mouthpieces and diadems made between 1400 and 1200 BC [2]. The opium poppy may be the inspiration behind the form of a particular type of juglet made in Base Ring ware between about 1650 and 1400 BC (see fig. 35b) and exported to Egypt, Syria and Palestine, since some certainly contained opium as shown by the analysis of the surviving contents. Opium can probably therefore be numbered among Cyprus's exports at this time. Laurel, one of many shrubs, was an important component of the wreaths regularly worn from the late sixth century BC onwards, as the statues show; some from a slightly earlier date also carry laurel branches.

The dense forests that covered the uplands – the whole of the Kyrenia mountain range and the lower slopes of Troodos – contained the Aleppo pine of Cyprus, the cedar and the cypress. All of these except the cedar (known from the fifth century BC onwards) have been identified in prehistoric contexts (before 1050 BC). The pine is the species mentioned by Theophrastus in the fourth century BC as one of the chief forest trees

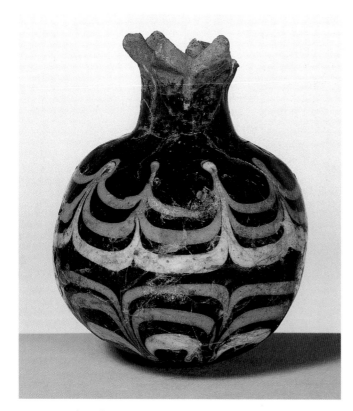

3 *Cypriot glass flask in the shape of a pomegranate formed around a core. With its short neck and pointed leaves it is a truer likeness of the fruit than the contemporary Egyptian glass examples. From Enkomi, 1400–1200 BC. Height 8.5 cm (3.3 in).*

used for ship-building. The olive, also indigenous, flourished throughout the hills and here too grew trees laden with fruit and nuts, notably pomegranates, figs, almonds and pistachios. The carob was probably introduced from the Yemen in the second century AD. Vines grew on the south-facing slopes of Troodos but on the higher peaks, above 1200 m (4000 ft), the oak and the Troodos pine predominated. Arrow-like patterns, which may represent conifers, and the occasional stylised, but more realistic, tree appear on painted vases of the later eighth and seventh centuries BC, but these apart the tree is seldom represented before the fifth century. Thereafter there are some accurate portrayals of trees (see fig. 95), some of which bear fruit. A fine illustration of the grape harvest appears on one of the mosaics of around AD 200 in the house of Dionysos at (New) Paphos.

The fruit most often depicted from an early date was the pomegranate, which with its numerous seeds may have been a symbol of fertility. The glass examples of the fourteenth to twelfth centuries BC [3], with their pointed calyx tips and short necks, are faithful representations of the fruit, unlike the contemporary Egyptian version. Gold pendants in the form of pomegranates (see fig. 59d) also date from the Late Bronze Age and pomegranates made of pottery decorate ring vases of the late second and early first millennia, while in the Iron Age they are made into children's rattles.

The rosette is one of the motifs that decorate funerary diadems and mouthpieces of gold in the Late Bronze Age, but it enjoyed its greatest popularity on painted vases from the beginning of the Iron Age until the sixth century BC and on stone reliefs of later dates, appearing in a number of forms. There is no reason to believe that it had any deep significance, and it is best seen as a purely decorative motif originally inspired by the designs on Syrian and Phoenician minor works of art and textiles. The lotus is another favourite plant motif of vase-painters during the earlier Iron Age, but it appears too on decorated metal bowls and other artefacts evidently made in Cyprus by resident Phoenician artisans or under strong north Syrian influence. Its origin, therefore, is not hard to find. Indeed, an earlier appearance is on a vessel of about 1600 BC made in a fabric of eastern inspiration, Bichrome wheel-made ware. The flower itself is the Egyptian water-lily of the Nile (*lotus nymphaea*) and the Egyptian depictions, which have three outer petals with the spaces filled with a varying number of smaller petals, are the truest representations. As a motif it appeared in the east in the earlier second millennium, where a rather more stylised 'north Syrian' version with two outer and one inner petal had been developed by the Iron Age. Many varieties of these two principal versions decorate Near Eastern ivories of the earlier first millennium, and the Cypriot artists are similarly ingenious. The lily, together with the date palm and lotus, is the inspiration behind the many representations of the 'tree of life' in Cypriot art, which are generally of eastern origin. The Greek version of the palmette is borrowed by artists mainly from the fifth century BC onwards, and of Greek origin also are the ivy leaf and acanthus which appear in Cypriot art from about the same time.

Certain species of wild animals have been identified as native to Cyprus. Of these the bones of the moufflon (wild sheep), together with those of the Persian fallow deer, wild pig, hare and fox have been found on prehistoric sites. A mosaic floor of around AD 200 in the *atrium* (courtyard) of the house of Dionysos at (New) Paphos shows hunting scenes;

4 *A moufflon followed by a hunting dog in a hunting scene on a mosaic of c.AD 200 in the eastern portico of the atrium (courtyard) of the house of Dionysos at (New) Paphos.*

among the conventional animals of the hunt are two moufflon [4], which must have been included to give local colour. The wild pig also appears in these scenes, but earlier portrayals by Cypriot artists include the occasional painted version on vases of the late eighth and early seventh centuries BC, terracotta models of the sixth century and a fine representation (of a boar) in relief on a limestone sarcophagus of about 470-460 BC (see fig. 95). The hedgehog is perhaps represented by a terracotta model of the thirteenth century BC imported from Greece. Lyre boxes were made of tortoise shells in the Iron Age.

With the first settlers came domesticated animals, including pigs, goats, sheep, dogs and cats. Cattle were apparently unknown before the second half of the third millennium and first appear in Cypriot art about 1900 BC. Thereafter it is the bull that receives most attention by artists, and it may have had a religious significance. Bulls' heads were set up on sticks like totem poles and bull-masks were worn by priests (and perhaps worshippers) in religious ceremonies (see fig. 73). Models of terracotta,

5 Above *Group of terracotta figurines: a pig, a stag and a bird. From Amathus and Kourion (Curium), 7th-6th century* BC. *Height of bird 8.4 cm (3.3 in).*

some made into vases, and earrings of gold wire threaded with bulls' heads (see fig. 59a) were made in the Bronze Age, and the bull was a favourite motif among vase painters of the later eighth and seventh centuries BC. The cattle of Geryon, captured by the hero Herakles, represented on a fine limestone relief of the second quarter of the fifth century BC, have humped backs and show a single horn, like the bull which appears with the boar on the limestone sarcophagus (above; see fig. 95). Oxen seem to have been used as draught animals in prehistoric times, a practice continued by the Romans. Remains of true horses have been found in contexts from about 1600 BC. Earlier equid bones are most probably those of donkeys or asses, which evidently acted as pack and draught animals, a role they played in later times as well. In the Iron Age lifelike horses are portrayed being ridden (see fig. 93) or drawing chariots. The terracotta models and painted vases of the Archaic period are again important sources of information about animal life and the way it is represented in Cypriot art [5]. Goats, stags and pigs are all portrayed. The goat and stag also appear on coins of the city-kingdoms, as does the ram. Terracotta children's rattles in the form of pigs of the Hellenistic and early Roman periods probably portray the domesticated rather than the wild species. Though certainly the home of the poisonous Levant viper, Cyprus seems hardly to have justified the title of Ophioussa (abode of snakes) which it acquired in late antiquity. Snakes figure in art from an early date [6], and are usually associated with the underworld (chthonic) deities. The Egyptian cobra (*uraeus*) was adopted as a decorative motif from about the

6 *Snakes and coils decorating a jug of Base Ring ware. From Maroni, 1650-1550* BC. *Height 27.4 cm (10.8 in).*

eighth century BC, originally perhaps reaching Cyprus by way of Syria and Phoenicia, although more direct influence may account for its appearance on the Egyptian crowns of some bronze statuettes.

The really fierce wild animals, tigers, panthers and lions, were not known in Cyprus. Of these the lion is most commonly portrayed and must, like representations of mythological beasts, owe much to outside contact and influence. In general these images were initially influenced by the products of Cyprus's eastern neighbours, notably in Syria and Phoenicia, which were also the source of the Egyptian features. From about the fifth century BC the representations usually show increasing dependence on Greek models.

Cyprus, being on the migration routes between Europe and Africa and Asia, is host to a great number of birds. The only indigenous species is the Cyprus warbler, but quite a few sub-species, including several songbirds, are also native to the island. Most conspicuous among the winter visitors today are aquatic birds, such as ducks, cranes, geese, swans and flamingos, and songbirds including

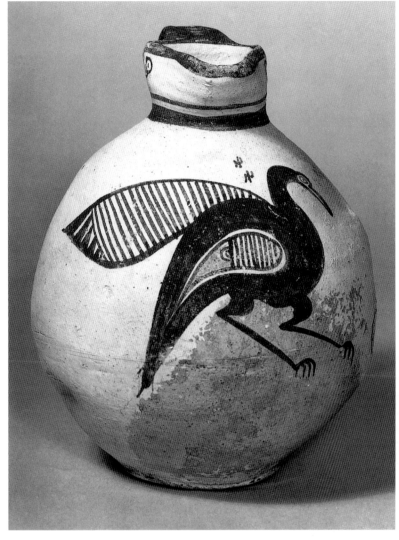

starlings, thrushes, larks and blackbirds. Eagles and vultures breed, and in the spring the nightingale arrives.

Few remains of birds have survived from antiquity and the representations in art, though common, are often not specific [7]. However, it seems that then, as now, vultures and eagles inhabited the mountainous regions, whereas ducks, swans, doves, partridges and songbirds were found in the fertile lowlands and marshlands.

Like the remains of birds, those of fish have seldom survived. Unlike birds, however, fish played an insignificant role in the artist's repertoire, except in the Archaic period when they are portrayed on some painted vases with pictorial scenes.

7 Bichrome ware jug decorated with an aquatic-looking bird in the 'free-field' pictorial style characteristic of southern and eastern Cyprus in the Archaic period, c. 700 BC. Height 18 cm (7.1 in).

Chapter Two | The historical background

U NTIL RECENTLY the first evidence for human occupation in Cyprus dated from around 7000 BC, comparatively late in comparison with that of its neighbours in Anatolia (Asia Minor) to the north, and Syria and Palestine to the east. Recent studies, however, suggest the presence of humans, albeit probably short-lived populations of groups of hunter-gatherers, some two or three thousand years earlier. Notably, in a cave at Akrotiri-Aetokremnos, on the south coast of Cyprus, hearths and chipped stone implements were found, together with bones of pygmy hippopotami and pygmy elephants as well as of birds and fish in a context dated to about 8800 BC. The earliest actual settlers probably arrived nearly two thousand years later from the Syro-Palestinian coast. They chose sites which were often conspicuous landmarks, with good arable land and an adequate water supply. Most were either on the coast or in river valleys with easy access to the sea. The communities were fairly scattered, mainly along the north coast and in the south. The economy was based on mixed farming, fishing or hunting. Pottery was not used, although unsuccessful experiments were made with untempered clay such as was used to line pits in the buildings. The culture, which takes its name from the best-known site of the period, Khirokitia, in the south, was short-lived. It seems to have gone into a decline, to have been finally extinguished by 5500 BC. This was followed

Map of Cyprus: ancient place names are italicised where they coincide with a modern village.

by a period of about a thousand years during which there seems to have been a break in the process of human settlement.

The second group of inhabitants had no connections with their predecessors, although they sometimes occupied the same sites. The culture (4600/4500-4000/3900 BC) is named after the extensively explored site of Sotira in the south. The people lived in agricultural villages which were comparatively short-lived; they maintained contact with each other but not with the outside world. By this time a flourishing ceramic industry had been born, establishing a tradition that has lasted to the present day. The demise of this culture appears to have been rapid, perhaps precipitated at least in some places by an earthquake, and several sites were abandoned. There ensues a gap in the archaeological record before the start of the succeeding era, which nevertheless reveals a number of linking features with the Sotira phase, as well as some critical changes.

The population of the succeeding era (4000/3900-2500 BC), known as the Chalcolithic period (literally, copper-stone age), was therefore not entirely new. The western end of the island was now more densely settled, and there were important innovations. Metal was used, though it was still uncommon, and a new type of miniature sculpture was produced [8]. Towards the end of the period new burial customs were practised, foreshadowing those of the Bronze Age. Around 2500 BC momentous changes took place in the north, which even now are not fully understood. Here the metalwork and pottery show strong affinities with that of southern Anatolia. It may be that refugees arrived from that area, fleeing from catastrophes that had befallen them around 2700/2600 BC. It is clear, however, that these changes did not occur throughout the island at the same time, but were initially concentrated at sites in the river valleys of the north-western central plain. This is known as the Philia culture.

Nevertheless Early Bronze Age culture, typified by the material from the cemetery at Vounous in the middle of the north coast, quite soon spread throughout the island. The availability of water and agricultural land still dictated the choice of sites. The transition to the Middle Bronze Age, about 1950 BC, was marked by no great upheaval, but for the first time there is evidence of indigenous copper mining, and tin bronze became industrially fashionable. Except for the most mountainous regions, the whole island was now occupied, but material culture was not uniform, being distinguished by pronounced regional variations. The construction of forts and the occurrence of mass burials towards the end of this period suggests the existence or threat of some internal disruption whose sources cannot be established with any degree of certainty, but no major catastrophe befell the whole island. In the seventeenth century BC Cyprus finally came out of its isolation. Goods were imported and Cypriot products reached Egypt and the Near East; society was becoming more urban, though communities still remained basically agrarian and inward-looking.

The Late Bronze Age (1650-1050 BC) was a period of great prosperity. The pattern of settlement underwent a significant change, with the development of coastal emporia which owed their existence and

8 *Picrolite (soft-stone) figurine shaped like a cross and wearing a necklace with a pendant of similar form. From Yialia, 3500-2500 BC. Height 15.3 cm (6 in).*

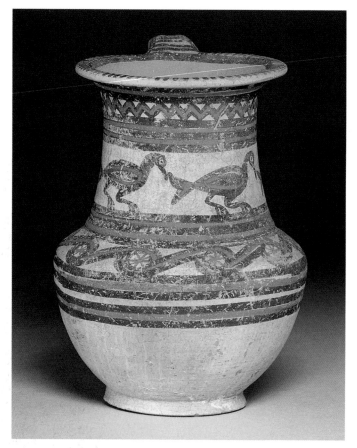

flourishing economies to intensified industry and commerce. From around 1500 BC, Cyprus enjoyed close trading contacts with the Near East [9], Egypt and the Greek world [10]. From this time dates the earliest evidence for Cypriot literacy, represented by the Cypro-Minoan script (see p. 80), and a century later the island became a major exporter of copper to the eastern Mediterranean region. Cyprus did not escape the disturbances that affected the entire Mediterranean world in the late thirteenth and early twelfth century BC. Bands of raiders, known as the 'Sea Peoples', were roaming the Mediterranean, and towards 1200 BC most of the principal towns of Mycenaean Greece were destroyed and abandoned. Some sites in Cyprus suffered violent destructions about the same time. The island, however, recovered. Life continued and prosperity returned, though now, in the twelfth century BC, most of the population lived in five large urban settlements.

The lively trade and contacts which Cyprus established around the eastern Mediterranean had a marked impact on her cultural expression, which owes debts not only to Syria and Palestine of the Levantine mainland, but also to the Aegean. The undeniable influence from Mycenaean Greece and Crete on writing, bronzework and sealstones of the twelfth century may have been due to the gradual and intermittent arrival of settlers from the Bronze Age Greek world. In other respects, however, the culture remained untouched by Greek influence. Burial cus-

9 Wheel-made jug decorated in red and black with birds and geometric motifs. One of a group of vessels which look distinctly Palestinian but whose shapes and linear ornaments mirror those of Cypriot White Painted ware. This Bichrome wheel-made ware was produced in workshops in eastern Cyprus between 1650 and 1450 BC. From Maroni. Height 21 cm (8.3 in).

10 An imported Mycenaean Greek silver bowl. The handle is not a true 'wishbone' and is therefore unlike those of contemporary Cypriot pottery vessels. Parallels for the shape can be found in Mycenaean bronzework. From Enkomi, 1400-1200 BC. Depth 20.7 cm (8.1 in).

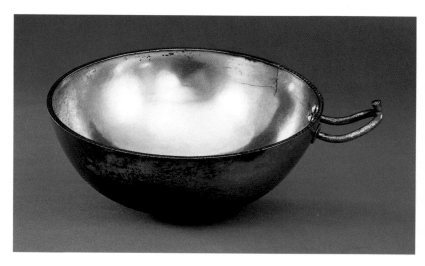

toms were unchanged and local Cypriot features permeate the ceramic industry; the weight systems continued to mirror those of the Near East and Egypt, and eastern influence is apparent in certain religious customs. Cypriot artisans continued to import luxury materials from the east (see fig. 38), while their own products showed a blend of Aegean, eastern and Cypriot elements as before. Immigration from the Bronze Age Greek world on a larger scale probably happened around 1100 BC. New Mycenaean Greek burial customs were practised in some eleventh-century cemeteries, and the Cypro-Minoan script of the Late Bronze Age died out, to be replaced for the most part by Cypro-Syllabic and the Greek language. Greek influence is apparent too in the pottery ware introduced around 1125 BC, in which everyday shapes are Aegean and only exotica (and plates of the succeeding White Painted ware) are of eastern origin.

By about 1050 BC iron had already been in use in Cyprus for about a century. The two hundred years between 1050 and 850 BC are usually described as a 'Dark Age', but even during this time contacts were maintained with both east and west, and jewellery and metalwork are evidence of some prosperity. In the eleventh century all but a few sites were abandoned, but gradually new settlements were established, for the most part on new sites. The revival in Cypriot culture in the mid-ninth century may be due to the arrival of Phoenician settlers, though some would place this two centuries earlier when close connections between the two countries began. 'Phoenician' metalwork and pottery (see figs 31, 41) were now made locally and Phoenician motifs adopted. There was strong interaction also between Cyprus and the states of north Syria.

The Archaic period (750-475 BC) was marked by a swift succession of foreign overlords: Assyria (*c*.707-612 BC), Egypt (*c*.570-526/5 BC) [11] and Persia (from 526/5 BC). Internally the island was organised into autonomous city-kingdoms; seven, and later ten, are mentioned in Assyrian documents. The first of these documents dates from about 707 BC, but how long it took for this political system to develop is not clear. Even the first settlers evidently had leaders in their communities, and the emporia of the Late Bronze Age must have developed quite a sophisticated political system, but there is no evidence of city-kingdoms at that time. Whether the Greeks had become the ruling class or not is difficult to determine, though seven out of ten of the Cypriot kings named in a prism of 663/2 BC of Esarhaddon, king of Assyria, have Greek names. Nevertheless, Phoenicians always ruled at Kition, and Phoenician political influence increased in the fifth century BC when a Phoenician dynasty ruled at Lapithos and a Phoenician exile even seized the throne of the most powerful (Greek) kingdom of Salamis for a short time. In the mid-fifth century Kition seized Idalion with Persian help, and in the fourth century it also acquired Tamassos and its copper mines, sold by its bankrupt last king. These city-kingdoms, whether ruled by Greeks, Phoenicians or native (Eteo-) Cypriots, as at Amathus, grew prosperous and had wide-ranging commercial connections. Towards the end of the sixth century BC they began to strike their own coinage. In 499/8 BC all the kingdoms of Cyprus, except for Amathus, joined with the East Greek

11 *Cypriot bronze statuette of a male worshipper. The impetus for the production of such strongly Egyptianising bronze statuettes in Cyprus seems to have come directly during the period of Egyptian rule. From the sanctuary of Apollo at Idalion, c.550 BC. Height 22 cm (8.7 in).*

cities of Ionia (part of modern Turkey) in the Ionian Revolt, an attempt to break away from Persian rule. This ended in failure. In the winter of 498/7 BC the cities of Cyprus, which had been holding out, were put to siege (see fig. 96) and eventually reduced by the Persians under King Darius I.

Throughout the Classical period (475-325 BC) Cyprus was poised between mainland Greece and Persia. The failure of the Ionian Revolt had left Persia firmly in control. Twenty years later the Cypriot cities were freed by an allied Greek fleet, but Persian rule soon reasserted itself, although the Athenian commander Cimon in 450/449 BC tried once more to secure the island as a Greek base. For forty years from 411 BC Cypriot politics were dominated by Evagoras I of Salamis, who was a great philhellene and openly welcomed all things Greek. By 391 BC, with the help

12 *Limestone statue of a female lyre-player in Greek dress, with her chiton (tunic) girded just below her breasts. Her features resemble those of Berenice I (c.340 to before 275 BC), the wife of Ptolemy II, King of Egypt and Cyprus. From Larnaca, early 3rd century BC. Height 55.5 cm (21.8 in).*

of Athens and Egypt, he controlled a large part of Cyprus. However, Athenian support was lost when, under the King's Peace (also known as the Peace of Antalkidas, the Spartan admiral) in 387/6 BC, the Athenians agreed to recognise Persian sovereignty over the cities of Asia and Cyprus. With Egypt as his only ally, Evagoras fought on against the Persians. He was eventually defeated in 380 BC, but negotiated a settlement under which he retained the throne of Salamis, while losing control over the rest of Cyprus. Evagoras I was murdered in 374/3 BC, and in the succeeding years the Cypriot cities fought among themselves, but Evagoras' successors continued the struggle against Persia. In 351 BC the Cypriot cities joined with Phoenicia and Egypt in another revolt against Persia, but this too was suppressed, and by 344/3 BC all the kingdoms of Cyprus were for a short time again under Persian control. However, Alexander the Great, king of Macedon and leader of the Greeks, had been gaining considerable successes against the Persian Empire. Following the Greek victory at the Battle of Issos in 333 BC, the Cypriot cities voluntarily submitted to Alexander. More than two hundred years of Persian overall control was finally brought to an end.

Following Alexander's death in 323 BC his generals, struggling to inherit his empire, used the island as a battleground and a number of the city-kingdoms were destroyed. In 294 BC Cyprus was annexed by Ptolemy, Alexander's general who had claimed Egypt. The city-kingdoms finally ceased to exist and the island became part of the large Hellenistic monarchy of Egypt. For the next two and a half centuries, apart from a short period in the second century BC, Cyprus remained in Ptolemaic hands. The island was organised as a military command under the overall control of a *strategos* (governor-general). All the *strategoi* and the other high officials including the city commandants were non-Cypriots, directly appointed by the king of Egypt. Certain democratic forms of internal administration were introduced, and in the third century BC some minor Phoenician dynasts were tolerated, at least at Lapithos in the north. The Ptolemies themselves were Macedonian Greeks, and so Cyprus became artistically orientated to the Hellenistic Greek world [12]. Although the island's natural resources, notably copper, corn and ship-building timber, were exploited for the benefit of the Egyptian kings, in return Cyprus enjoyed comparative peace, broken occasionally by attacks from the Seleucid kings of Syria. In 58 BC Cyprus was first annexed by Rome, now a major force in the eastern Mediterranean. During the civil wars of the Roman Republic Cyprus was returned to the Ptolemies of Egypt by Julius Caesar, who gave the island to his mistress, Cleopatra VII. In 36 BC the gift was confirmed by Mark Antony, then Cleopatra's husband. However, in 30 BC Octavian, later to be Augustus, the first Roman emperor, took Alexandria, the Egyptian capital. Cleopatra committed suicide, and Cyprus reverted to Rome.

Together with Cilicia on the southern coast of Asia Minor (modern Turkey), the island was at first incorporated in the province of Syria. In 22 BC Cyprus was detached from Syria and became a Senatorial Province. Thereafter, until the reorganisation of the Empire about three hundred years later, the island was ruled by governors of senatorial rank, appointed annually and given the title of Proconsul. Administration was organised in four districts – Paphos in the west, Amathus in the south, Salamis in the east and Lapithos in the north. There were twelve or thirteen cities and Paphos was the capital, as it had been since early in the second century BC [13]. Like the Ptolemies, the Romans exploited the island's natural resources to enrich their own coffers. As part of the Roman east, the civilisation remained basically Greek. In the late third century AD the emperor Diocletian began reorganising the Empire. This process was continued by Constantine the Great, and Cyprus was assigned to the most easterly of the twelve dioceses that were created. In AD 330 Byzantium, renamed Constantinople (modern Istanbul), replaced Rome as the capital of the Roman Empire. On the division of the Roman Empire in AD 395 Cyprus was allocated to the eastern half. This, and the establishment of Christianity as the official religion about the same time, opened a new era in the island's history.

13 *Portrait of the Roman emperor Vespasian (AD 69-79) on a bronze sestertius struck by the Koinon of Cypriot cities. The reverse shows Zeus of Salamis (fig. 86).*

Chapter Three | Architecture and mosaics

THE FIRST SETTLERS (of the Khirokitia culture, 7000/6500-5700/5500 BC) lived in round huts of rubble and mudbrick, used alone or together, with flat roofs and windows [14]. Some houses had two concentric walls. The living area, in which there were hearths (for cooking and heating) and benches, was small and restricted by supporting piers which were occasionally painted, as were some walls and floors. Such painted decoration seems to be confined to more important buildings. Some of the dwellings had radial divisions formed of stones and river pebbles. The houses were generally close together but, nevertheless, there were open spaces in the villages that suggest some community gatherings. This circular architecture contrasts with the mainland to the east where at this time rectilinear plans were the norm. In the succeeding Sotira period (4600/4500-4000/3900 BC) house plans tended towards the rectangular, but they were still single-room dwellings. A predilection for subterranean living is suggested by a settlement at Ayios Epiktetos-Vrysi on a northern coastal promontory, where groups of six or more irregular-shaped structures are wedged in hollows, their roofs well below ground. Further inland at Philia a network of underground tunnels may have been used for storage. The Chalcolithic era (4000/3900-2500 BC) saw continued interest in the subterranean, but, more importantly,

14 *The remains of a house at Khirokitia with rubble walls. Inside are the lower parts of supporting piers.*

increased sophistication in building with stone and, at Kissonerga Mosphilia near Paphos in the west, three buildings seem to have had official functions. One of these has a red-stained floor as well as radial divisions.

In the Early and Middle Bronze Age (2300-1650 BC), single structures were replaced by multi-roomed buildings. Individual units usually had two rooms (sometimes subdivided), one for habitation and one for storage, reached from a corridor or perhaps an open space in front. At Alambra, a site on the copper belt, the buildings were aligned along a street reminiscent of towns on the Asiatic mainland. In the seventeenth century BC, fortresses were built mainly along the edges of the central plain and in the Karpass peninsula. Their purpose is unknown, but they may signify local unrest; most are too far from the coast to be a response to sea-raiders. They vary considerably in plan. The best known, at Nitovikla, is a square fortress with a massive gateway flanked by square towers around a central court, like contemporary forts in Syria and Anatolia.

Ashlar blocks – drafted blocks of stone – were used in the gateway at Nitovikla. This building technique [15] was brought to Cyprus from Syria, but it was to be another two or three centuries before big buildings of ashlar blocks were established in the Cypriot countryside to accompany new planned towns marking the urbanisation of the island. These buildings, most of which date from the thirteenth century BC, evidently had official functions. Exactly what these were is not always easy to determine, though one (of three) at Kalavassos-Ayios Dhimitrios was used for oil production. This building was aligned along a street. The best evidence we have for town planning of this period is at Enkomi [16], one of the coastal emporia of the Late Bronze Age (silting has caused a change in the coastline). Here the streets cross each other at right angles providing a grid plan, and the twelfth-century town at Hala Sultan Tekké was laid out the same way. Similar grid plans are attested in Egypt

15 *View of part of the 'sanctuary of the horned god' at Enkomi. It was built of fine ashlar masonry about 1200 BC.*

16 *Plan of the excavated area of Enkomi showing the location of the industrial quarters* [1], *the 'sanctuary of the ingot god'* [2] *and the 'sanctuary of the horned god'* [3]. *Enough has been discovered to reveal the overall grid plan of the city.*

from the third millennium and there is a hint of a grid plan in the four-teenth- and thirteenth-century city at Ugarit (home for some Cypriots) on the Syrian coast just opposite Enkomi, but most Near Eastern sites have been insufficiently explored to reveal their plans. Houses had several rooms, which at Enkomi were grouped around a central courtyard. Bathrooms had cemented floors and Enkomi had lavatories as well as an elaborate drainage system. Clay bathtubs have been found there and elsewhere. Sanctuaries are discussed in chapter 8, but it is worth noting that ashlar was not used in their construction before 1200 BC.

Little is known about the architecture of the first centuries of the Iron Age, though in the eleventh and tenth centuries ashlar was repaired by rubble. Phoenician masons may have been responsible for building a columned hall in one of the Late Bronze Age sanctuaries at Kition in the ninth century, which was rebuilt after a fire in about 800 BC. In front of the central door were bases for two free-standing pillars, recalling those of Jachin and Boaz in King Solomon's temple. The ability of Cypriot architects and masons of the Archaic period (750-475 BC) is well illustrated by built tombs described in chapter 8. Domestic buildings were less sophisticated, and generally constructed of mudbrick on rubble foundations set in mud-mortar. Rooms were rectangular or apsidal. Public buildings were once again built of fine ashlar masonry, with mud-mortar. At Tamassos some structures in a sanctuary within the walled city were of wood; Phoenician influence is apparent in the half-column capitals, supported by wooden shafts, as it is in the architectural decoration of some built tombs and in some sanctuary plans (see p. 63). To the sixth century belong some Greek architectural fragments, but the evidence for Greek temples or public buildings is very slight. Volute capitals, some showing a 'tree of life', and lotus capitals, of the late seventh to fifth centuries BC, often crowned votive or funerary columns or pilasters. However, they were used architecturally in shrine models, and volute capitals acted as door jambs in one of the built tombs at Tamassos and were used in other structures there and at Salamis. Iconographically Cypriot Hathor capitals [17] of the sixth and fifth centuries BC owe much to eastern and Greek inspiration, but outside Cyprus actual capitals are exclusive to Egypt, where they have a long history. Again several Cypriot examples evidently crowned votive monuments, but their architectural use has been confirmed by a discovery in the palace at Amathus.

Palaces of Cypriot kings have been identified at Soloi, Vouni, Idalion and (Old) Paphos as well as Amathus. Only the overall plan of Vouni [18] can be reconstructed, but generally it seems that Cypriot

17 Above right *Upper part of a votive Hathor capital from near the palace at Amathus. Both sides show the head of the Egyptian goddess Hathor, who in Cyprus came to be equated with Aphrodite, supporting a shrine. Traces of rich polychrome decoration are preserved; c.480 BC. Height as shown 118.2 cm (46.5 in).*

18 Below *The central court of the palace at Vouni. At the back a magnificent staircase leads to the state apartments. Originally built between about 500 and 450 BC, the palace was rebuilt in the later fifth century when a second court, flanked by storerooms and apartments, was added on the south-east and the entrance was made more imposing.*

palace builders of the sixth and fifth centuries followed Mesopotamian and Achaemenid Persian models, as did architects in other satrapies of the Persian Empire. White gypsum plaster covered some of the walls that were often built of ashlar blocks with a rubble core cemented with gypsum plaster. Structures in the Classical sanctuary of Aphrodite and Cybele at Tamassos had doors and windows framed with wall plaster painted in red and maroon. Here the walls were initially built of sandstone ashlar blocks cemented with gypsum plaster, but later dry-laid limestone blocks were used. Roof tiles of Greek Corinthian type have been found, but it seems likely that some roofs and ceilings were made of cane and, at least at Idalion, covered with gypsum plaster. Private houses were more modest, usually built of mudbrick on stone foundations, but Phoenician influence is apparent at Carpasia, a flourishing harbour town on the north of the Karpass. The walls were constructed of rubble on ashlar foundations with square blocks at the angles and as uprights along the walls at intervals, a technique derived from timber-framed buildings, and known in the Phoenician homeland and at the Phoenician colony at Motya in Sicily. Kition had an elaborate sewage system and ship-sheds in the harbour.

19 *Floor mosaic of about 300 BC from a Hellenistic building under the house of Dionysos at (New) Paphos showing the legendary sea-monster Scylla, part human, part dog and part fish. It is made mainly of black and white pebbles, with reddish-brown pebbles used for Scylla's hair and the trident and mast she holds. Once a beautiful girl, Scylla was turned into this creature by a jealous rival and thereafter spent her time sinking ships in the Sicilian sea.*

Many of the public and domestic buildings of the Hellenistic period (325-30 BC) have been obliterated by the earthquakes of 15 BC and AD 76/7 and by later Roman structures, but epigraphic evidence records gymnasia (where loyalty to the Ptolemaic regime was focused) at Salamis, Kition and Kourion. The theatre at Kourion was originally built in the second century BC on a Greek plan with an *orchestra* (dancing place) greater than a semi-circle and a high *proskenion* (stage building) supported by half-columns. The theatre at Priene in Ionia (modern Turkey) is a good parallel. Recent work at (New) Paphos has confirmed that the theatre, the largest in Cyprus, was originally built in the late fourth century BC soon after the foundation of the city by Nikokles, the last king of Paphos. Public buildings were generally constructed of ashlar masonry, while those with two storeys usually had a superstructure of mudbrick on thick foundation walls with an outer face of ashlar blocks revetting a mud backing and an inner rubble core. At Soloi walls of the palace, no doubt the home of a Ptolemaic official, were decorated with painted stucco as were buildings at Alexandria, the capital of Egypt. A palatial building with porticoes and an open courtyard and columns of the Ionian and Doric orders on the Fanari hill at (New) Paphos has been compared with other palaces of the Hellenistic world. Roof tiles of the period have been found in quantity on the island of Geronisos. As Hellenistic cities elsewhere, notably on the west coast of Asia Minor (modern Turkey), (New) Paphos at least, and no doubt other Hellenistic cities of Cyprus, were planned on a grid system with particular functions assigned to different districts. Greek architectural fragments include Corinthian capitals, and Doric and Ionic mouldings (the latter sometimes of limestone). Private houses were usually rather modest with rectangular rooms, though at Ayia Irini, where the architecture was again modelled on timber-framed buildings, the houses have bathrooms and small workshops. Towards the end of the period some houses have rooms arranged around a colonnaded courtyard, anticipating Roman designs. Bands of colour may decorate the walls, and frescos in some tombs showing garlands, like those decorating houses on the island of Delos, and with the walls painted to imitate alabaster in the Egyptian manner, give some idea of the painted designs that may have adorned Cypriot Hellenistic houses. From (New) Paphos, the island's capital from the second century BC, comes the first mosaic floor from Cyprus [19], composed, like earlier Greek examples, mainly of black and white pebbles. Dating from about 300 BC, it shows the forepart of the legendary Scylla. A second mosaic of this type from Kourion, showing a hydra with fish, is of the third century BC, and one with a geometric design decorates the floor of a circular bath house near the *agora* (market-place) at Amathus (that in a similar bath house at Kourion is probably Roman, as it has irregular cubes of stone with the pebbles). Contemporary parallels are known from Asia Minor (modern Turkey). In the first century BC the first mosaic (from Kition) composed entirely of little cubes of stone cut specially for the purpose (*tesserae*) was made. It retains the limited black-and-white colour scheme of the pebble mosaics, but the more flexible medium allows for more imaginative patterns.

20 *View of the northern part of the city of Salamis with remains of public buildings of the Roman period. In the centre is the gymnasium with a colonnaded palaestra (wrestling ground) and a bath building on its seaward side.*

21 Above *View of the Roman theatre at Soloi. The semi-circular cavea (seating) has been cut out of the rock and there is an orchestra (dancing place) with a rectangular stage building at its rear. The floor of the orchestra was plastered with lime cement over a rubble substructure. The theatre could hold 3500 spectators.*

22 *The partly reconstructed temple, originally built c.AD 100, in the sanctuary of Apollo Hylates at Curium (Kourion). The columns are crowned by Nabataean capitals.*

Roman Cyprus, like other Roman provinces all over the Empire, had cities, some twelve or thirteen, connected by an efficient road system, and having imposing public buildings often grouped together to form a city centre [20]. These buildings included market-places, gymnasia, public baths, theatres [21] (some later converted, according to Roman taste, for hunting or aquatic games), amphitheatres for gladiatorial contests, and *nymphaea* (fountain houses). Other typical Roman buildings include an Odeion (small theatre) and Asklepieion (temple dedicated to Asklepios, god of medicine) at (New) Paphos, the island's capital until the second half of the fourth century AD. Aqueducts ensured a good water supply. For the most part the impetus for Cypriot architects came from the eastern Roman Empire, notably Syria and Asia Minor (modern Turkey). Nabataean capitals of the 'pseudo-Corinthian' type, best known at Petra (Jordan) of the Hellenistic kingdom of Nabataea, crown capitals of the temples of Greco-Roman type of the first and second century AD in the redesigned sanctuaries at Kourion [22] and Amathus, and one was found reused at Salamis (along with Nabataean pottery). In the early Roman period such capitals are known from other sites in Jordan as well as Petra, from Baalbek in inland Phoenicia and from the Egyptian Fayum, and could have reached Cyprus from the east or Egypt.

Most Roman houses in Cyprus followed the traditional plan of rooms grouped around a central (colonnaded) courtyard. The majority are of modest size, but liberally decorated with mosaic floors. One particularly large house at Paphos with more than one hundred rooms, known as the house of Theseus after the scene of Theseus and the Minotaur in a mosaic made in the late third and restored in the fourth century AD [23], may have belonged to the Roman pro-consul. (New) Paphos was perhaps the centre of mosaic production in Cyprus, but mosaic floors are not exclusively found there. It is in the eastern orbit of the Roman Empire that the Cypriot mosaics belong. They show close links with the mosaics of the Syro-Palestinian coast and to some extent those of southern Asia Minor (modern Turkey). There are some striking par-

23 *Detail showing the upper part of Theseus, named in Greek, from a floor mosaic in a room in the south wing of the house of Theseus at (New) Paphos. Accompanying Theseus are depictions of the Minotaur and Ariadne as well as personifications of Crete and the labyrinth, and the whole is surrounded by a meander pattern, perhaps symbolic of the labyrinth. Originally made in the late 3rd century AD, it was restored a century later following earthquake damage.*

27

24 *Floor mosaic showing a peacock with its train fully spread, from a room next to the main entrance of the house of Dionysos at (New) Paphos. The peacock is framed by a band with a wavy ribbon and surrounded by mosaics showing polychrome geometric patterns; c.AD 200.*

allels such as the gladiators named in Greek in mosaics of AD 250-300 from the house of the gladiators at Kourion, exactly as in mosaics from the island of Kos. Of all the buildings in Cyprus, the house of Dionysos at (New) Paphos has the best preserved mosaic floors in fifteen of the rooms closest to the *atrium* (central court). They date from around AD 200. The house takes its name from the Dionysiac procession (the triumph of Dionysos) in the *tablinum* (main reception room), and other mythological themes include Phaedra and Hippolytos, the rape of Ganymede, Pyramos and Thisbe, Ikarios, the first man to make wine, Dionysos with an inscription in Greek ('the first wine-drinkers'), and

Apollo and Daphne. There is also a hunting scene; a depiction of the common Roman theme of the four seasons with inscriptions reading 'welcome' and 'you too', appropriate in a room that was apparently the main entrance; and a magnificent peacock [24], as well as several floors with geometric patterns. The walls of the living rooms and corridors were once richly decorated with paintings, and parts of coloured fresco decoration of the late third centry AD, showing mythological scenes, survive in the gymnasium baths at Salamis. A coin of Licinius I (AD 317-23) was found in the bedding mortar of the mosaics in the dining room of the house of Aion (who is the subject of the central panel), also at (New) Paphos. Inscriptions (in Greek) identify the personages in the scenes showing the birth of Dionysos; a Dionysiac procession, again illustrating the god's triumph; the judgement of Marsyas [25]; Leda and the Swan and the beauty contest, presided over by Aion, between Cassiopeia and the Nereids. Artistically of the highest quality, rich in design and colour, the iconography is of particular interest. These mosaics were made in the later fourth century AD when Christianity became the official religion of the Roman Empire, but, as in other secular buildings of the time, they depict pagan scenes.

25 *Floor mosaic showing Apollo and Marsyas from the triclinium (dining room) of the house of Aion at (New) Paphos. Marsyas, who dared to compete with his double flute against the heavenly sounds of Apollo's lyre, is dragged away at the left. Apollo is seated on the right with Olympus, Marsyas' son and pupil, begging for mercy at his feet. Between Apollo and Marsyas stands Plane, evidently a personification of the 'erring mind' that led Marsyas to his fate; c.AD 325-50.*

Chapter Four | Island of copper

CYPRUS WAS RENOWNED for copper in antiquity and, indeed, the very word 'copper' comes from the Roman name for the metal, *Cyprium aes* (literally 'copper of Cyprus'). Earlier, the name Ku-pi-ri-yo appears in Mycenaean Greek texts and we hear of the Kyproi in the poems of Homer. The principal copper-bearing ores are on the north and north-east slopes of the Troodos mountains. Less frequently they occur in the southern foothills. Discoveries in the mines at Ambelikou, in the northern foothills to the west of Nicosia, show that here the copper deposits were exploited in the nineteenth century BC. At the same time there was considerable metallurgical activity in the nearby settlement at Aletri. This is, as yet, the first archaeological evidence for copper-mining and metalworking in Cyprus but, as we shall see, an earlier date for these activities is suggested by the copper and bronze items that were produced from the middle of the third millennium.

At present the earliest metal objects date from soon after 4000 BC and a few more belong to the years between about 3000 and 2500 BC. These are not numerous but nevertheless significant since they indicate a knowledge of metalworking and justify giving the title of Chalcolithic ('copper-stone') to that era. All may be made of native copper, which is found in a pure form on the surface of the earth. The technology that led to their manufacture was probably a local development.

Copper ore must have been mined and then smelted to release the metal to produce the many copper and bronze tools and weapons (see fig. 91) typical of Cyprus in the Early as well as the Middle Bronze Age. The first of the series were made around 2500 BC. Many early utensils are of arsenical copper (either a natural mixture of arsenic and copper, or the product of deliberate alloying). Although arsenic was poisonous and difficult to use, it was not replaced by tin in Cyprus before the nineteenth century BC. Even after this, tin-bronze was not universal. Copper (and not bronze) remained the preferred material for weapons for another three hundred years. Tin probably reached Cyprus via Syria from a source as yet undiscovered. It is still unclear how the Cypriots learnt to make bronze by combining copper with a small amount of arsenic or tin. The answer must lie in the interpretation of the events that ushered in the Cypriot Bronze Age. This new metal technology was perhaps introduced by refugees from Anatolia escaping from the disturbances which marked the end of the Early Bronze II period in that area about 2700/2600 BC, but did not become common until the beginning of the second millennium BC.

After a spectacular start there is little change in Cypriot metalwork until about 1600 BC, and many of the types even survived for another century and a half. Typical of this early series are weapons with hooked (rat-tail) tangs (see fig. 91). The tang was inserted into a handle, the form of which may have been similar to those of the terracotta models [26]. The blade was probably cast in a one-piece mould and then ham-

26 *Pottery model of a metal dagger (or knife) with a wooden handle and a leather sheath. Made of Red Polished ware which has been blackened (except at the points) in the firing process and decorated with incised linear patterns. Probably made in northern Cyprus, c.2075-2000 BC. Length of dagger 17.3 cm (6.8 in).*

mered. The same type of weapon appears in many different sizes, and the function of a particular item is usually determined by its size, rather an arbitrary means of classification. Swords, dirks, daggers and spearheads are all represented. Among the tools are axes, chisels, awls, drills and punches. Common are flat wedge-shaped axes, which were cast in one-piece moulds and presumably set in slots on the long axis of the handles. To the Middle Bronze Age (c.1950-1650 BC) belong axes of a Near Eastern type with long blades and cylindrical ribbed sockets for the handles. The technical skill required in their manufacture is not otherwise known in Cyprus before the late thirteenth or twelfth century BC. All those found in Cyprus are remarkably like each other and yet slightly different from their eastern prototypes. It therefore seems probable that they were made locally by a foreign smith who perhaps brought the moulds with him. Dress-pins of several varieties have been found, often in pairs, but there is little real evidence to show how they were worn. Those with a hole in the shaft are known as toggle pins. Other personal objects are tweezers and razors.

Excavations have revealed increasing metallurgical activity on settlement sites in the Late Bronze Age. Nearly all the major centres, including Enkomi, Kition, Hala Sultan Tekké, (Old) Paphos and Maroni, provide evidence for copper-smelting, as do smaller settlements including Alassa near Episkopi. Some such as Kalavassos-Ayios Dhimitrios apparently owed their existence to the mining and working of copper. This is the time too of the correspondence between the king of a country referred to as Alashiya and the pharaoh. The letters are clay tablets inscribed in the cuneiform (wedge-shaped) script of western Asia and the language is Akkadian. They are of the second quarter of the fourteenth century BC and were found in the palace of Akhenaten at el-Amarna in Upper Egypt. In several of them the king promises the pharaoh copper, and asks in return for gifts of silver and luxury goods, such as a bedstead of ebony inlaid with gold and a gold chariot. References to Alashiya or Asy occur in other Near Eastern documents from Egypt, Syria and Anatolia. The earliest is of the eighteenth century and the latest of the twelfth century BC. From these we learn that Alashiya supplied copper to Syria and Anatolia in return for finished articles. The country had a sea-coast and, besides a king, it had its own fleet in the late thirteenth century BC. In the twelfth century BC it was overcome by the 'Sea Peoples', bands of adventurers roaming the Mediterranean. Earlier, in the fourteenth century, it was an ally of Egypt and an enemy of the Hittites, who were then struggling to gain control over Syria. Debate has raged over the location of Alashiya (or Asy) ever since it was first identified as Cyprus in 1895. Today many scholars would support such an identification, though some suggest it refers to a single site such as Enkomi rather than the whole island. There are, however, major stumbling blocks, among them the language and script used by the king of Alashiya – on present evidence the Cypriot script at this time was Cypro-Minoan but, as it is undeciphered, the language is unknown.

Whatever the answer to the Alashiya problem, Cyprus's role in the copper trade in the Late Bronze Age is not easy to assess. A ship containing a vast number of copper ingots, among other items, sank off the south coast of Turkey at Uluburun (Kaş) at the end of the fourteenth century BC. Most scholars believe that the ship was sailing towards the Aegean, and certain specialists, but not all, maintain that at least some of the ingots are of Cypriot copper. This is supported by some ingots from Crete of about this time shown by analysis to be of Cypriot copper (earlier Cretan ingots are not of Cypriot copper). Also of Cypriot origin

27 Bronze four-sided stand with ajouré (openwork) decoration showing on each side a man approaching a 'tree'. Here the man is carrying an ingot shaped like an oxhide, the form in which copper was transported, whether within a country or overseas. Perhaps from Kourion (Curium), 12th century BC. Height 11 cm (4.3 in).

are copper ingots found in a shipwreck of about 1200 BC from Cape Gelidonya in Turkey. Latest scientific evidence suggests that Cyprus began exporting copper ingots to both the eastern and western Mediterranean only after 1400 BC, but individual objects fashioned by the island's metalworkers may have reached overseas destinations earlier in the Late Bronze Age.

The products of Cypriot metalworkers in the Late Bronze Age were at first (until about 1450 BC) steeped in the old traditions. Little new influence from east or west is apparent in either the techniques or the designs. Only from the area of the Bay of Morphou come a few bronze items of apparently Minoan (Cretan) origin. These were found along with vessels from Minoan Crete and Mycenaean Greece, which suggests, perhaps, some isolated connection between the Aegean and that part of Cyprus alone. In spite of industrial evidence from many of the settlement sites, there is little bronzework from securely dated contexts in Cyprus after around 1450 until late in the thirteenth century BC.

It was probably at about this time, towards the end of the Late Bronze Age, that the Cypriot industry was transformed under foreign influence. Many of the innovations had their origins in Mycenaean Greece but others came from Egypt or the Near East. Techniques previously very rare or completely unknown were practised. These included elaborate work in sheet metal to form vessels, which now became much more common; casting in a two-piece mould to make tools with a central socket for the handle; lost-wax casting of statuettes and lead-filled weights in the form of animals [28] or human heads, and hard soldering to join together parts of tripods and other vessel stands that had been made in separate pieces. These last, including some that were cast in one piece, are technical masterpieces produced in Cypriot workshops, mainly between the late thirteenth and mid-twelfth centuries BC. The decoration is partly in the *ajouré* (openwork) technique [27], and the designs show a blend of Aegean and Near Eastern elements. They travelled westwards to Greece and the Aegean islands and even to Italy, where they seem to have survived to be dedicated as heirlooms between the eleventh and seventh centuries BC.

The exact date of this revolution in the Cypriot bronze industry is difficult to determine, but much of the evidence comes from hoards which were deposited in the twelfth century BC. Among these is the 'foundry hoard' [29], which was found at Enkomi in 1897, probably in the north-western part of the site. Unfortunately no precise records were made at the time of its discovery and a complete inventory is lacking. Nevertheless, the hoard appears to be the contents of a smithy comprising the smith's own tools and new tools for carpentry and agricultural work. Other articles, such as weapons and vessel stands, were presumably for sale. Fragmentary vessels, stands, weapons and the waste left

28 Above *Bronze weight in the form of a bull, partially filled with lead. It weighs one Egyptian deben and was perhaps made in Egypt. Its findspot suggests it dates from the Archaic period, though most weights of this type from Cyprus belong to the late 13th or 12th centuries BC. From the sanctuary of Apollo at Idalion.*
Length 4.8 cm (1.9 in).

29 Right *Bronze smithy tools from the Enkomi 'foundry hoard': a furnace spatula for managing red-hot charcoal, a charcoal shovel and a pair of tongs; 12th century BC. Length of shovel 52.3 cm (20.6 in).*

30 Above *Bronze fibula (brooch). This typically Cypriot type of the early Iron Age spread eastwards, and westwards even to Spain, where local copies were made; c.7th century* BC. *Length 18.5 cm (7.3 in).*

31 Right *Bronze lampstand: the lamp rested on the ring between the 'arms' supported by the column decorated with lotus flowers. Such lampstands were probably made by Phoenician artisans resident in Cyprus; c.8th century* BC. *Height 26.4 cm (10.4 in).*

over from the casting process are all scrap metal, which must have been set aside for remelting. The ingots are unworked copper; the only complete example is shaped like an oxhide, and this is the form in which copper was transported, whether within the island or overseas.

Much bronzework has been found in early Iron Age Cyprus. Of Cypriot origin and manufacture are *fibulae* (brooches) [30] with triangular bows strengthened with wire and beads and bowls whose handles are decorated with lotus flowers. Both these types spread eastwards and westwards from Cyprus. The *fibulae* reached Palestine, Greece, Sardinia and even Spain, where they were imitated locally, while the bowls travelled to the Near East, Greece and Italy. Phoenician immigrants were probably responsible for lampstands [31] and some of the metal bowls decorated with intricate scenes. The bronze harness and horse trappings and the vessels from the tombs of the aristocrats at Salamis were imported from or influenced by different parts of the Near East. Continued industrial activity is apparent from the discovery of copper workshops at Kition and Tamassos and recently at Ayia Varvara in the Nicosia district. The first were in use from about 650 to 450 BC, and the latter two from about 600 BC into the Hellenistic period.

Copper was one of the principal attractions of Cyprus to the Ptolemies and the Romans. The Ptolemies themselves took over control of the mines, putting an official called an *anti-strategos* ('lieutenant-

32 *Bronze head of a youth. It was probably cast abroad in southern Asia Minor but the modelling of the head may have been carried out elsewhere, perhaps in Cyprus. From Soloi, mid-2nd century AD. Height 25.5 cm (10 in).*

general') in charge. Like almost all high officials, he would have been a non-Cypriot directly appointed by the king of Egypt. Large bronze statues were certainly cast hollow by the lost-wax process in Cyprus from about the first century BC. A bronze foundry of the late Hellenistic or early Roman period was found in Cyprus in the house of Dionysos at (New) Paphos. Cypriot bronzework of this period is for the most part indistinguishable from that produced elsewhere in the Mediterranean world. Among the artefacts were surgical instruments, toilet articles and statuettes. Even the bronze portraits so far discovered on the island were apparently cast abroad, probably in southern Asia Minor. However, the modelling of the face of a head from Soloi of the mid-second century AD [32] may have been carried out in Cyprus. Like the Ptolemies, the Romans obtained for themselves the direct benefit from the copper mines. Their working was farmed out to contractors under the central control of a Roman procurator. (In 12 BC half the production of the Soloi mines was leased to Herod of Judaea.) Nevertheless, the island must have profited from the presence of such a large-scale industrial enterprise.

Chapter Five | Trade and manufacture

G EOGRAPHICAL POSITION alone ensured Cyprus's role as a major trading post in antiquity. Tucked in the eastern corner of the Mediterranean, the island lies at the crossroads of seaborne trade between the ancient civilisations of Anatolia to the north, Egypt to the south, Greece and Rome to the west and Mesopotamia and Persia to the east [33]. Then, as now, its strategic importance did not go unnoticed. Cyprus was subjected to foreign rule, fought over and used as a battleground. At different times the island was a major supplier to the ancient world of copper, corn and timber for ship-building. In its own right Cyprus was a manufacturing centre and, using native resources as well as imported materials, produced highly individual works of art and various artefacts. We are fortunate that many pottery vessels have survived from ancient Cyprus. Many of these vases were made locally and illustrate the ingenuity of Cypriot potters throughout antiquity. Others were imported from different parts of the Mediterranean world. These in particular help to provide a picture of the island's trading contacts and their consequences.

Overseas trade was not properly established for a long time after the arrival of the earliest settlers. If the first Neolithic colonists who

33 Divers excavating the stern of a Greek merchant ship which sank off the coast at Kyrenia at the end of the 4th century BC. The cargo included amphorae from Rhodes containing wine, and others from Samos filled with oil, millstones (for ballast) from the island of Nisyros and 10,000 almonds which had probably just been collected from Cyprus.

established the Neolithic culture came from the nearby Syrian coast around 7000 BC, it is likely that they brought with them the more exotic materials, such as obsidian (originally from south-central Anatolia), cornelian and mother-of-pearl, that have been found at their settlement sites. They did not make pottery, but used andesite, a grey-green stone obtainable from the river-beds, for their vases and figurines. Sickle blades and arrow-heads of flint were made to support their farming economy.

In the later Neolithic period (4600/4500-4000/3900 BC) handmade pottery was produced in Cyprus. In the north designs were painted in red on a white ground, sometimes using a brush with multiple heads; in the south patterns were made by 'combing' the slip (a specially prepared clay solution used for coating vessels) with a tool with multiple teeth.

The hallmarks of the Chalcolithic period (4000/3900-2500 BC) — the advent of metal, the cruciform figurines and the new burial customs — are all discussed in other chapters. Red-on-White painted pottery, now produced in the south as well as the north, continued the earlier tradition, but towards the end of the period some monochrome vessels were made. Their final colour depended on the firing conditions in a manner foreshadowing practices of the Bronze Age.

There are unmistakable south Anatolian traits in the Cypriot products of the succeeding era, which ushered in the Bronze Age, notably in the pottery and metal forms. Red Polished [34] became the dominant pottery ware lasting into the Middle Bronze Age. The vessels

34 Three vessels of Red Polished ware with incised decoration: a) a jug with a double cut-away beaked spout from Alambra; b) a deep tulip-shaped bowl with lug handles from Vounous; c) a round-mouthed jug. The deep bowl is two-coloured, being black on the rim and the interior, and the incisions of the beaked jug are filled with white paint. Early and Middle Bronze Age, 2300-1650 BC. Height of beaked jug 29.8 cm (11.7 in).

were still handmade and covered by a slip, which was burnished and then often decorated with patterns incised with a sharp cutting edge before being fired. The final colour of the slip, and so the appearance of the vessel, depended on the amount of iron oxide in the solution (more was needed for it to become red, less for black), and the conditions and temperature of firing. By exercising tight control over the cooling as well as the firing conditions, potters were able to produce vessels that were either mottled or two-coloured. The latter were often mainly red on the outside but black on the exterior of the rim and the inside. Favourite shapes were shallow bowls and round-bottomed jugs, either with beaked 'cut-away' spouts or tall necks with round flaring mouths. More elaborate items produced in this fabric included human and animal figurines and deep bowls with various attachments.

Some painted pottery was produced in the Early Bronze Age but the start of the Middle Bronze Age, around 1950 BC, is marked by the beginning of a new tradition of painted wares. The handmade vessels were carefully burnished. The decoration of linear patterns in reddish brown or dark brown on a light ground gave the ware its name, White Painted (see fig. 48). Analysis of the decoration has made it possible to distinguish certain regional styles. In the east of the island, for example, straight or wavy lines set vertically or at an angle so as to cross each other were popular, while in the north the pattern structure was more formal. Brushes with multiple heads were used more frequently in eastern Cyprus, notably on the Karpass peninsula, which was the home of another painted ware, Red-on-Black (or Red-on-Red); the designs were painted in red on a black (or red) ground. In the south and extreme west of the island, monochrome vases continued to be made although without incised decoration.

It was during the Early and Middle Bronze Age that Cyprus was beginning to emerge from its isolation. In the seventeenth century BC contacts began to be established with Crete and subsequently Greece as well as with the Near East (Syria and Palestine), Egypt and, towards the end of the period, southern Anatolia.

35 a) *A dish with a wishbone handle;* b) *a juglet which, if turned upside down, resembles an opium poppy. Of Base Ring ware (the juglet decorated with white painted lines), such vessels were widely exported. The dish, from Phoenikiais or Alambra, was made between 1550 and 1450 BC, and the juglet (also from Cyprus) is of 1650-1500 BC. Height of juglet 14.6 cm (5.7 in).*

In the early stages of the Late Bronze Age (*c*.1650-1450 BC), Cypriot civilisation was for the most part deeply rooted in its past, most apparent from the bronzework and other smaller artefacts. Base Ring and White Slip became the dominant wares of fine pottery into the twelfth century BC. Significantly, both were handmade in the old tradition. Base Ring takes its name from the ring-shaped bases applied to nearly every vessel in the group. The vases have unusually thin walls, normally covered by a highly polished brown slip. The decoration, if any, consists of relief bands and white painted lines. The most common shapes are jugs with tall necks and flaring mouths, little jugs (or juglets) and bowls with 'wishbone' handles [35]. The juglets may have been inspired by an inverted poppy head and used as containers for opium (see p. 7). It is likely too that the bodies were made in moulds. Whatever the truth of the opium hypothesis, the juglets and also the dishes with wishbone

36 *Two vessels of* White Slip *ware:* a) *a 'milk bowl' (with a true wishbone handle);* b) *a tankard. The latter is decorated with fine lines in two colours, not a very common technique for this ware, which was widely exported, particularly the milk bowls. Both pieces were found in Cyprus, the tankard at Maroni, and were made between 1650 and 1450 BC. Height of tankard 20.2 cm (8 in).*

handles were exported to the Aegean, Egypt, Syria and Palestine. The thick white slip which covers the vessels of White Slip ware [36] would have been very pure. This was painted with linear patterns in orange, brown or black, or occasionally in two colours. Round-bottomed bowls with wishbone handles, known as 'milk bowls', were widely exported to the east but presumably for their aesthetic value rather than their contents, since they could not be sealed.

The creativity of Cypriot potters at this time is best exemplified by the way in which foreign techniques and styles were adapted to the local idiom. Until the beginning of the Late Bronze Age all ceramic products were made by hand, without the benefit of the fast wheel, but the introduction of this new method of pottery manufacture, which had been in use for centuries among the island's neighbours, resulted in the appearance of a number of novel ceramic series. Two of the most distinctive were Bichrome wheel-made ware (1650-1450 BC), in which geometric and floral patterns and figured scenes were painted in red and black, and Red Lustrous wheel-made ware (1600-1200 BC), which was used for a number of elegant and unusual shapes, such as vessels in the forms of human arms, spindle bottles and pilgrim flasks. Long thought to have been produced in Anatolia, Syria, Palestine or Egypt, where these

37 *Faience vessel in the form of a closed lotus flower decorated with the Egyptian god of infinity, Heb, holding lotus flowers. Made in Egypt, 1350-1150 BC. From Enkomi. Height 22.3 cm (8.8 in).*

two wares are well attested, they have been shown by recent research to have also been made in Cyprus and exported.

The pottery production, therefore, illustrates Cyprus's close relations with the Near East and Egypt from early in the Late Bronze Age. In the fourteenth and thirteenth centuries BC urban centres including Enkomi, Kition, Hala Sultan Tekké, Maroni and (Old) Paphos (several of them established shortly before 1600 BC) enjoyed great prosperity. Materials including gold, ivory and faience [37] and some finished articles were imported. Cypriot workshops made jewellery, sealstones and artefacts of glass, faience and ivory. Their products show an amalgam of local and foreign influences and are of a high technical quality. Some contacts were established with Italy, Sicily and Sardinia. Cypriots were actually living at Ugarit on the Syrian coast. From there probably came the original inspiration for the construction of buildings with fine ashlar blocks, a tradition which continued in Cyprus in the twelfth century BC and in the Iron Age.

Also during the fourteenth and most of the thirteenth centuries a great quantity of pottery was imported by Cyprus from Mycenaean Greece. These Mycenaean vessels are all wheel-made, usually of fine clay covered by a creamy-buff slip on which the designs were painted in glossy brown (it sometimes turned to red on firing). Particularly popular in Cyprus were large vessels such as *amphorae* (storage jars) and *kraters* (bowls for mixing wine and water) decorated with processions of chariots, bulls and birds [39]. At the same time Cyprus was exporting copper to the Aegean and beyond and may have also been supplying perishables such as grain, textiles or timber. Some fine Cypriot pottery has been found in the Greek world, but very few other artefacts. It is likely that trade was in the hands of independent entrepreneurs who plied the routes, setting up and putting down goods wherever profit was to be made. In that way they could dispense with the need to balance the books precisely between different countries.

Towards the end of the thirteenth century BC the supply of Mycenaean pottery dwindled. In response to this, Cypriot potters started to make their own imitations and so, at last, generally adopted the fast wheel. For a short time, until about 1200 BC, some vases, usually bell-shaped *kraters*, bore pictorial decoration, often of bulls or goats executed in a 'rude' or 'pastoral' style. Longer-lasting and still produced in the twelfth century BC were shallow dishes (and a few other shapes) with linear designs.

Cyprus was caught up in the tribulations that affected the whole Mediterranean world at this time. Its own twelfth-century civilisation enjoyed a certain amount of prosperity. Strong influence from Mycenaean Greece and Crete is apparent, particularly on some pottery, bronzework and sealstones, but the jewellery, faience and ivory work [38] owe much to the Near East. The whole is, as before, an amalgam of Cypriot, Aegean and eastern elements. Relations with the far west were intensified and some Cypriot bronzeworkers went abroad to settle and work in Sicily and Sardinia.

38 Above *Ivory gaming box decorated with hunting scenes and animals. The squares on the top of the box are arranged for the Egyptian game of twenty squares; underneath is a drawer for the gaming pieces. Found at Enkomi and made in the 12th century* BC. *It was probably carved in Cyprus from ivory imported from Syria or Egypt. Length 29.1 cm (11.5 in).*

39 Left *Mycenaean vessel (amphoroid krater) decorated with a procession of chariots. Many vessels decorated in this pictorial style have been found in Cyprus and they were perhaps made in Mycenaean Greece particularly for export. From near Maroni, 14th century* BC. *Height 41.9 cm (16.5 in).*

Around 1125 BC a new pottery ware, Proto-White Painted, was first made by Cypriot potters. Since its shapes and ornaments are mostly of Greek origin and it is the forerunner of the principal Iron Age fabric, it may speak for the arrival of Greeks already in the twelfth century BC. Specifically Cretan (but modified and adapted) are certain forms, including the straight-sided box (*pyxis*), *kalathos* (basket-like vase) and a particular type of flask shaped like a bird. Influence from Syria and Palestine accounts for certain shapes and motifs. Sometimes designs were painted in two colours, recalling the technique of some White Slip vessels [36b].

Although groups of settlers from the Greek world may have arrived intermittently in Cyprus during the twelfth century BC, the most massive migrations probably happened around 1100 BC. It is in cemeteries of the eleventh century BC that tombs of the Mycenaean

40 *Flask of White Painted ware in the form of a bird. The bird shape for flasks was introduced to Cyprus from Crete and appears in the Cypriot pottery repertoire from around 1125 BC. This example was made between about 1050 and 1000 BC. Length 22 cm (8.7 in).*

Greek type occur alongside the traditional Cypriot graves (see p. 71) and only then did the Cypro-Minoan script finally die out. Ironworking had been practised in Cyprus from around 1150 BC, and it was probably from Cyprus that the new technology was introduced to Greece in the early eleventh century. This also points to close contacts between the two areas at the time. The jewellery, principally of eastern types, and the metalwork continuing the Aegean tradition, found with pottery in the first half of the eleventh century, are evidence of some prosperity.

Even during the first two hundred years of the Iron Age (1050-850 BC), normally described as a 'Dark Age', some contacts were maintained with both east and west. The most common fine pottery is White Painted, with the ornaments in black or brown on a buff or greenish-white slip [40]. This had its origins in the fabric produced at the very end of the Late Bronze Age. New influence from Syria and Palestine accounts for the reappearance of Bichrome ware which has in addition broad areas painted in matt red. New shapes at this period of eastern origin are plates and a barrel-shaped jug with a ridge opposite the handle, inspired by a type of bottle made earlier in Syria and Palestine. Some of the decorative motifs, such as schematic birds, have their origin in Late

Bronze Age Crete, but others, including wild goats, the 'tree of life' and circle patterns, are of eastern inspiration.

An upturn in Cypriot culture in the mid-ninth century seems to have been due to the arrival of Phoenician settlers, though some say that Phoenician immigrants first arrived two centuries earlier when close contacts were established between the two countries. Typical Phoenician pottery, both Red Slip (the vases are covered by a red coating) and Black-on-Red (with black ornaments on the red ground), had been imported earlier, but it was henceforth locally made as well [41]. The shapes in the local repertoire included some of Phoenician origin, such as deep bowls with linear decoration and flat-bottomed juglets with bands around the belly and concentric circles on the shoulders. Others imitated those in the contemporary White Painted and Bichrome fabrics, which in turn were also made in the 'Phoenician' shapes. Overall the standard of Cypriot potting improved greatly. Ornaments were more carefully drawn, and further attempts were made at a purely pictorial style.

Greek pottery from Athens and Euboea had started arriving in Cyprus around 950 BC. By the late tenth century Cypriot exports had reached Euboea, where it seems likely that the local bronze industry was revived under Cypriot tuition. From the mid-ninth century, the volume of imported Greek pottery increased. In the eighth century some may have been brought by Euboeans on their way to the Syrian coast, since at that time Cyprus and Euboea were apparently sharing the trade with Al Mina in north Syria (modern Turkey). Copies of Euboean vases were also made locally by Cypriot potters. Crete received a number of eastern and eastern-inspired goods between the tenth and eighth centuries, all of which probably travelled by way of Cyprus. Cyprus's own pottery reached Crete from the late ninth century. Crete was in fact one of the three islands, the others being Rhodes and Kos, that received a steady supply of Cypriot pottery starting soon after Phoenicians settled at Kition around 850 BC. Many of these exports were slow-pouring Black-on-Red perfume jugs. They were imitated locally in the eighth century BC, perhaps to contain perfume produced in small factories set up and staffed by Phoenicians from Cyprus.

The Archaic period had begun about 750 BC, and this (lasting until 475 BC) was another era of great prosperity for Cyprus, notwithstanding its domination by three foreign powers (Assyria c.707-612 BC, Egypt

41 *A jug and a perfume flask of Black-on-Red ware, both from Amathus and made in Cyprus. The jug with its flat bottom is a Phoenician shape, while the perfume flask is an example of the type exported to some Greek islands and closely imitated in Crete. The ridge for the handle was used by Cypriot potters at the beginning of the Iron Age for jugs with barrel-shaped bodies; 800-750 BC. Height of flask 13.4 cm (5.3 in).*

c.570-526/5 BC and then Persia from 526/5 BC). The island had wide-ranging commercial contacts and played an increasingly important role in international trade. A number of artefacts of Near Eastern origin, imported or imitated by the Cypriots, reached not only the Greek world but also Phoenician centres in the western Mediterranean. Direct contacts were maintained with Syria and Phoenicia, while Phoenician immigrants in Cyprus were probably responsible for the production of some fine metalwork (see fig. 31), and at least one sculpture. Small terracotta figures in the Phoenician tradition were produced such as pregnant women, women holding their breasts and some chariot models, and Phoenician dedications were made in the sanctuary at (Old) Paphos destroyed for the Persian siege ramp in 498/7 BC (see fig. 96). Within the Greek world Cyprus's relations were principally with the East Greek cities established on the west coast of Asia Minor and the neighbouring islands. East Greek pottery was imported and some attempts were made to imitate it locally. Cypriot goods were exported, notably to Samos, Rhodes and Euboea. It was to sanctuary sites in this same area, as well as elsewhere in the Aegean, in Phoenicia and at Naucratis in Egypt, that a prolific class of Cypriot limestone statuettes was exported, or made locally by itinerant Cypriot sculptors (of Cypriot stone), between about 620/610 and 550 BC. Closer contacts were established with Egypt during the period of its rule. In Cyprus itself signs of Egyptian influence at this time include stone representations of the Egyptian god Ammon, a painted burial chamber at Salamis, a dedication to the goddess Isis and, to my mind, the production of strongly Egyptianising bronze statuettes (see fig. 11) and Hathor capitals (see fig. 17). Around 700 BC a Cypriot dedication was made at the 'international' shrine at Delphi, the first evidence of an association that was to last into the second century AD.

The inclusion of Cyprus in the Persian Empire in 526/5 BC brought the island into closer contact with the East Greek cities of Asia Minor (modern Turkey), which had suffered the same fate. Athens had, however, now won all the foreign markets for pottery and so the Greek pottery in Cyprus, as elsewhere, is mainly Attic (Athenian). This resulted in some imitation by Cypriot potters and also in some Attic vases being made in Cypriot shapes, apparently specifically aimed at the Cypriot market.

The political organisation of the island into autonomous city-kingdoms led to the development of regional styles, stimulated to some extent by the swift succession of foreign overlords. Regionalism

42 Ox-shaped flask (askos) of Black-on-Red ware decorated with circles and linear patterns, a typical product of a western Cypriot pottery workshop in the Archaic period. From Kourion (Curium), 750-600 BC. Height 19.0 cm (7.5 in).

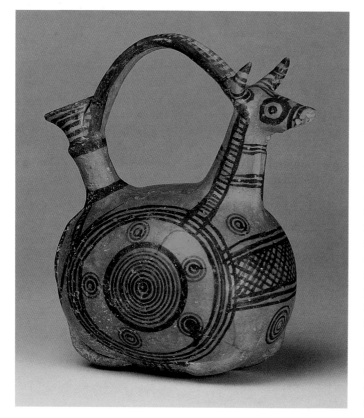

is particularly apparent in the pottery, although the wares remained the same as in the previous period and the shapes were generally developed from those of their precursors. The attractive pictorial style (see fig. 7) became characteristic of the south and east. A wide variety of scenes were depicted, drawing their inspiration mainly from Syrian and Phoenician textiles (see fig. 50) and minor art, such as ivory carvings, decorated metalwork and sealstones. In the north and west potters concentrated on producing intricate shapes with elaborate circle patterns [42]. The pottery of Amathus has close-packed decoration.

The Classical period (about 475–325 BC) found Cyprus poised between Greece and Persia. Persia increased its control after the failure of the Ionian Revolt, an attempt by the East Greek cities of Asia Minor to free themselves from Persian rule, in which the Cypriot cities participated. Athens made some attempts to liberate the island in the first half of the fifth century BC (see p. 16). Attic pottery continued to dominate the market, and inspiration from Classical Greece is apparent in several media. Phoenician influence spread within the island. Lapithos and Marion had Phoenician kings in the fifth century; Kition acquired the kingdom of Idalion around 450 BC (and a century later the kingdom of Tamassos). Soon after the mid-fifth century BC the Phoenicians had even established a dynasty at Salamis, a traditionally Greek city. However, for the forty years after his seizure of the throne at Salamis in about 411 BC the Greek Cypriot Evagoras I dominated Cypriot politics and openly welcomed Greek imports and immigrants. A colony of Salaminians was established in Athens and in the late fourth century the Kitians established a shrine in the Athenian port of Piraeus.

Greek influence therefore permeated certain Cypriot products of the fifth and fourth centuries BC, although eastern influence is still apparent and the Cypriot character survived. In pottery the same fabrics were employed. Bichrome Red, which adds decoration in white to the traditional Black-on-Red, had occasionally been known earlier but now became more popular. The vessels were generally taller and slimmer. A few new types were introduced, among them a jug with a *kore* (Greek maiden) on the neck holding a smaller jug, which acts as a spout [43]. Greek ornaments were copied. A few attempts were made to imitate the Greek red-figure technique with the decoration reserved (i.e., in the colour of the clay) against a dark background and with the details painted. Contacts with Syria and Phoenicia were maintained. Cypriot sculpture was exported, while imports from Phoenicia included mummy-shaped sarcophagi (see p. 73), which were imitated by the Phoenicians at Kition. Phoenician building techniques were sometimes employed. Cyprus obviously had relations with the ruling power, though Persian

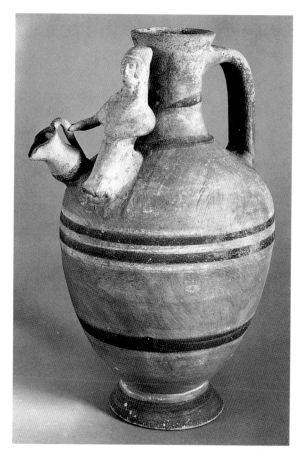

43 *Pitcher of Bichrome Red ware with patterns in white as well as black on the red ground. The figure of a woman of Greek type sits on the shoulder pouring from a small jug. From Marion, 5th century BC. Height 32.3 cm (12.7 in).*

influence on its civilisation is restricted to the plans of certain buildings (or 'palaces') and a few shapes and ornaments mostly for items of precious metal.

Although Alexander the Great released the Cypriot kingdoms from Persian control in 333 BC, he also took away some of their autonomy, and when the island was annexed by Ptolemy of Egypt in 294 BC they finally ceased to exist. Cyprus became part of the large Hellenistic state of Egypt. As such it became artistically orientated to the Hellenistic world and its own products in general conform to the cosmopolitan styles of the period. As the island was now part of the Greek world, its athletes took part in the Panathenaic and Olympic games and sculptors from Salamis worked at Delphi and at Lindos in Rhodes. Cyprus maintained particularly close ties with Egypt, shown by sculpture in the Ptolemaic style (see fig. 12) as well as burial customs and architectural features (see fig. 78) that reflect fashions in the newly founded Egyptian city of Alexandria. Fine glasses and pottery were imported from Syria and Asia Minor, but Cyprus's own workshops were very active. Glassmaking was revived, with the manufacture of small *amphorae* with S-shaped handles, formed of coloured glass around a removable core [44a], and small pendants in the form of female heads made by a similar technique. The earlier White Painted and Plain White fabrics survived, but Cypriot workshops also made versions of the common Greek black glaze (vases covered by a glossy black slip), including some with moulded, impressed or white painted decoration, and the red slip wares of Asia Minor. Mould-made lamps [44d] were produced in local workshops, but the jewellery, terracotta figurines, bronzework and other small artefacts conform to the types found throughout the Hellenistic world.

44 *Pottery and glass of the Hellenistic period found in Cyprus and dating from the 3rd to the 1st century BC:* a) *a core-formed glass scent bottle with S-shaped handles, made in Cyprus;* b) *a skyphos (cup) with white painted decoration, perhaps made in Cyprus;* c) *a Grey ware bowl (drinking cup), perhaps made in Asia Minor;* d) *a clay lamp, made in Cyprus;* e) *a lagynos (wine-jug) decorated with fishes and possibly made in Cyprus. Height of lagynos 17.8 cm (7 in).*

Under Roman rule Cyprus came fully under the influence of the civilisation of the Empire, which especially in the east was rooted in Hellenistic traditions. Consequently the language and culture of the island remained basically Greek. The predominant fine pottery of the earlier Roman period was a fabric covered by a glossy red slip. It was locally produced, the shapes mainly copying the vases of Syria and southern Asia Minor. Dishes, bowls and jugs found a ready market in Cyprus. Many vessels had a low foot, and jugs often had angled handles. This local Red Slip ware became particularly widespread within Cyprus from the first century AD [45b,i]. It was widely exported in the east in the second century, and the occasional piece reached the west. Potters at (New) Paphos apparently had direct links with the west; many vessels of the first and second century AD imported from Campania in southern Italy have been found in the house of Dionysos. Vases with a lead glaze were imported from Tarsus in southern Asia Minor, and a few vessels came from Egypt. The glass industry throughout the Roman world was transformed by the invention of glass-blowing in the mid-first century BC. Previously a luxury product, glass now became much more widely available. Workshops producing the common blown glasses were established in Cyprus [45c], as they were elsewhere in the Roman Empire. Favourite shapes of the Cypriot glass-blowers were jars, beakers and flasks for oil or perfume. Some of the jars had the lid decorated with a design enamelled on the inside so as to be viewed through the glass [45d,g]. Cypriot glassware was exported to the Black Sea, the Greek world and northern Italy, but the more elaborate vessels were still imported, principally from Syrian glasshouses. Skilled artisans working in Cyprus were responsible for a fine series of mosaics (see figs 4, 23, 24, 25, 97). Sculptors, bronze-workers and jewellers remained active, though specifically Cypriot products are often difficult to identify. Cyprus had become an integral part of the Roman east with its basically Greek language and culture, which were to have a profound influence on her later history.

45 *Pottery and glass of the Roman period found in Cyprus and probably made there:* a) *a clay lamp;* b) *a Red Slip ware wine-jug;* c) *a blown-glass bottle for oil or perfume;* d) *a blown-glass bowl with enamelled lid;* e) *a Red Slip ware bowl;* f) *a White ware wine-jug with decoration resembling that of glasses with wheel-cut patterns;* g) *a blown-glass lid with a figure of Eros painted on the inside;* h) *a clay lamp signed on the bottom by a Cypriot lamp-maker;* i) *a Red Slip ware wine-jug. Most of these pieces date between the 1st and 2nd centuries AD, although the signed lamp is of the 3rd-4th century. Height of tallest jug 22.8 cm (9 in).*

Chapter Six | The human form in Cypriot art

THE HUMAN FORM appeared in the art of the earliest inhabitants of Cyprus and remained a dominant theme throughout antiquity. With a few exceptions the figures of the Neolithic period were quite small, no more than 19 cm (7.5 in) in height, and made of stone; they are rather elementary representations of the human form, with the arms and legs reduced to mere stumps. The latest examples of this type [46] are contemporary with another variety (see fig. 8) typical of the succeeding Chalcolithic era (4000/3900-2500 BC). Shaped like a cross, almost invariably made of soft stone (bluish-green picrolite or serpentine), this type has now been shown to have developed within Cyprus from the stump-like form. The cruciform category includes some figures of terracotta. An interesting repertoire in that material shows the ingenuity of the Chalcolithic artists.

46 Left *Limestone female figurine whose arms and legs are mere stumps. She is the largest example of this type known at present (36 cm/14.2 in tall) and the material is also unusual. Found in the debris of a destroyed building at Lemba-Lakkous, she is known as the 'Lemba Lady'. She must have been a fertility charm and may even represent a goddess; c.2500 BC.*

48 Below *Vessels of White Painted ware of the Middle and beginning of the Late Bronze Age, late 18th-16th century BC: a bottle with a human figure growing out of it, probably from Idalion; a bottle in quasi-human form; a boat with a human figure sitting on its edge; a jug with a human figure on the shoulder. Height of jug 21 cm (8.3 in).*

47 Above *Plank-shaped figure of White Painted ware, the upper part of an exceptionally large example; 1725-1625 BC. Height 17 cm (6.7 in).*

Bronze Age representations differ from their predecessors in both style and the preferred material. In the Early and Middle phases (2300-1650 BC) plank-shaped figurines of terracotta predominate. Made in fabrics akin to those of the contemporary pottery, Red Polished (see fig. 67) and White Painted [47], they bear incised or painted decoration. The most typical have a rectangular body on which is placed a narrower and smaller rectangle for the head and neck. Some pieces have two heads. Red Polished examples have incised patterns indicating headbands, necklaces, belts and facial features. Some of either fabric have modelled noses or small ears and perhaps crudely formed breasts; they may cradle a child in their arms. The great majority of these are quite small, between about 18 and 26 cm (7.1 and 10.2 in) tall, which emphasises how exceptionally large the White Painted example illustrated here [47] must have been, since the surviving head and neck already measure 17 cm (6.7 in). This is perhaps an example of another plank-shaped type, which has the head and body of roughly the same width, so that there are no real shoulders. Others are in the form of 'combs' or 'brushes': they have long thin necks and square bodies, often decorated on the lower half with vertical incised lines. Since some Chalcolithic examples of this type made of picrolite are now known, it may be that the plank-shaped type, like the cruciform variety, developed in Cyprus itself. It cannot, however, be denied that such figurines (of terracotta) were being produced in southern Anatolia at the time and this was perhaps one of the new and foreign ideas from that region that helped to usher in the Bronze Age to Cyprus.

Early and Middle Bronze Age potters seldom included representations of human beings in the incised or painted decoration on their vases, but were nevertheless happy to model them in clay: figures sit on the edges of bowls, grow out of them or are formed out of the pots themselves [48]. They are simply made, with solid bodies and schematic heads and arms; terracotta models show similar figures taking part in various activities. There are scarcely any human figures in stone of this period and indeed only a very few among all the terracotta examples are depicted fully in the round.

At the end of the Middle Bronze Age, though continuing to work in clay, artists made radical changes in the way they represented human figures. They are now obviously female, having a curving rather than straight outline, with wide hips and an incised pubic triangle. They are usually portrayed standing with their hands held just below their breasts [49]. This type of figurine

49 *Two female figurines of terracotta with their hands below their breasts. One wears a flat cap squashing down the ears; the ears of the other are large and pierced and adorned with earrings. Both from Enkomi, c.1450-1200 BC. Height of example with cap 21.3 cm (8.4 in).*

originated in the east in the third millennium BC and reached Cyprus by way of Syria. Closest to their Syrian prototypes are those with large flanged ears, sometimes adorned with earrings. A second variety has a flattened head with the ears apparently squashed down by a hat, perhaps a sign of Mycenaean Greek influence.

While the prehistoric representations of the human form can be classified into broad groups in a roughly chronological succession, Iron Age portrayals are more diverse. The greatest innovation was the production of large-scale (life-size or even larger) statues in stone, terracotta and, more rarely, bronze. This happened in Cyprus around the middle of the seventh century BC. Smaller (less than life-size) statuettes were produced in similar styles in the same materials. Vast numbers of yet smaller figures of terracotta in various techniques and types were also made. Many of these figures, both large and small, were dedicated in sanctuaries, and it seems that the major shrines had their own workshops ready to supply visiting pilgrims. In the Hellenistic and more particularly the Roman period, statues of rulers and gods were set up in public places and adorned municipal buildings. Painted and model representations decorate pottery vessels, and others are included in the designs on sealstones and on metal vessels and utensils.

The two-dimensional representations of the earlier Iron Age generally portray eastern figures. This is hardly surprising, since the painted vases were inspired by Syrian and Phoenician textiles and minor art, such as ivories, metalwork and seals [50]. In addition, a number of the metal bowls and other artefacts were most probably made by Phoenician artisans resident in Cyprus. The women usually have their hair in a plain mass, often combed into a bun at the nape of the neck and sometimes with a curling lock falling forward by the ear. They wear long plain robes, often of patterned material. The men, if not in Egyptian costume of crown and kilt, are usually dressed and equipped as warriors with conical helmets and large round shields.

Until about 475 BC small terracotta figurines often had trumpet-shaped or conical bodies (see fig. 70). The solid pieces were handmade, but some of the hollow ones were formed on a wheel. Less common are examples with bell-shaped wheel-made bodies, sometimes with detachable legs. The arms were simply modelled and might be upraised, hold an object close to the body or, for the women, hold the breasts. At first all heads were handmade. They were peg-like, with prominent noses and with the top often formed into a hat, a pointed 'bonnet' (or helmet) for the men and a rectangular crown (polos) for the women. From the seventh or sixth century BC moulds, originally introduced from the east, were in widespread use by Cypriot coroplasts. The head alone or the whole figure might be made in a mould, and this heralds a notable change in style. The women now have more delicate features, often with wig-like hair. If the body too is moulded, the back is flat and the costume either

50 *Interior of a bowl of Bichrome ware decorated with pairs of women; they wear long robes, with their hair falling down to the nape of the neck, and stand on either side of 'lotus flower' trees, sniffing flowers. From Achna, 6th century BC. Depth 34.3 cm (13.5 in).*

a transparent tunic or a robe of thicker material with a sash (see fig. 74a), beneath a cloak pulled up over the head. The men too become more life-like, and wear a wide variety of caps and helmets. Their normal dress is a long plain robe and a mantle.

Cypriot sculptors in the Iron Age worked either in terracotta or locally available stone of different varieties, all commonly called 'lime-stone'. The large terracotta statues were often handmade in separate pieces and then joined together, though the faces were normally made in a mould. The stone was relatively soft, lending itself to engraved and painted decoration rather than sharply carved detail. A particular characteristic of Cypriot limestone sculpture, which survived into the Hellenistic period, was that the backs of the statues were generally ignored, being left completely or virtually flat with no attempt to show details of the anatomy. Throughout antiquity marble was imported, at first in the fifth century BC from Greece, later also from Asia Minor (modern Turkey). A few finished statues of marble had reached Cyprus from Greece as early as the sixth century BC.

The earliest style of Iron Age Cypriot sculpture was essentially a local creation, although it shows some eastern influence. The faces are triangular or oval, the expressions severe and the eyes large and prominent, sometimes with 'feathered' eyebrows (they are decorated with hatched lines). The men sport beards, usually rounded and protruding, and wear helmets or conical bonnets. The women are bedecked with jewellery and their headdress is a turban or low crown. The usual dress for men and women, similar to that worn by moulded terracottas, is an ankle-length robe (see fig. 74b), partly covered by a cloak for the men. Both men and women stand with their feet together; the left arm is usually by the side and the right bent across the body, the women's holding an offering and the men's tucked in a fold of the cloak. By the early sixth century BC Cyprus came into contact with other Mediterranean powers. This led to the development of a new style which reflects influence from Egypt and the Greek east (the Greek cities on the coast of Asia Minor and the neighbouring islands), as well as the Near East. The hair is now usually arranged in an Egyptian-type *klaft* (wig) [51], and in East Greek style the features are softer, with a hint of a smile on the lips. The men continue to sport beards, which are often long and square, like those of their earlier Assyrian rulers, and rendered in long narrow

51 *Limestone head from a statue of a bearded worshipper with his hair arranged in an Egyptian-style klaft (wig) plaited with strings. From the sanctuary of Apollo at Idalion, c.550 BC. Height 41 cm (16.1 in).*

52 Above *Painted terracotta head from a statue of a worshipper, looking like an Assyrian with his long square beard. From the sanctuary of Apollo at Phrangissa, Tamassos, about 590-580 BC. Height 36 cm (14.2 in).*

53 Above right *Terracotta figure of a female harp-player; she is bedecked with jewellery and her hair is arranged in spiral curls. From the sanctuary of Apollo at Idalion, early 6th century BC. Height 30.7 cm (12.1 in).*

strands which may be decorated with oblique lines [52], or curled at the end; other beards are shorter and rounded, or more pointed, and sometimes formed of curls. 'Feathered' eyebrows are still quite common. They wear a variety of helmets, mostly of Near Eastern types, or conical bonnets. Besides the eastern long robe and mantle, a loin-cloth, perhaps of Greek origin, and a headband may be worn. The women's costume and headdress are virtually unchanged (see fig. 74c), and they continue to be bedecked with jewellery. Some have the Egyptian *klaft*, often covered by a veil, but for others the hair is arranged in elaborate spiral curls [53] familiar from Syrian and Phoenician ivory work.

In 526/5 BC Cyprus suffered the same fate as the East Greek cities on the west coast of Asia Minor (modern Turkey) of being absorbed into the Persian Empire which, after the fall of Babylon to the Great King in the autumn of 539 BC, had also included Syria and Phoenicia. Freedom of movement within the Empire intensified contact between the areas. Cypriot sculptors became more dependent on East Greek models and influenced by Phoenician taste. Figures of men now normally wear a linen *chiton* (tunic) and a woollen *himation* (cloak), the typical dress of the East Greek school, and stand with one foot advanced [55], like their models. Only occasionally are they naked in the mainland Greek tradition, although this form was occasionally adopted by Cypriot sculptors already in the early sixth century BC. Some are clean-shaven, but others retain their beards, which are now regularly artificially curled. Similar curls appear on the back of the neck of some of those with long hair, who may keep their oriental helmets or Egyptian crowns, but others adopt the Greek short hairstyle, with curls over the forehead secured by a wreath. Stimulated in part by the resident Phoenician population, some sculptures wear Egyptian crowns and kilts reflecting a Phoenician fashion for Egyptianising statues. All now have softer, more rounded features and a distinct smile. The women have similar features and some continue to wear the traditional dress, but there are also some faithful copies of Greek *korai* (maidens), with their drapery falling in elaborate folds and long hair arranged in decorative patterns. The Cypriot versions keep their rich jewellery.

From 475 to 325 BC the political situation brought Cyprus into closer contact with mainland Greece. For representations of the human form this led to increasing Cypriot dependence on Greek models. There remain, however, some distinctly Cypriot limestone statues and statuettes. They continue the tradition established at the end of the sixth century [54]: the men wear Greek costume and may have beards, perhaps

55 *Limestone statue of a male worshipper carrying a bird as an offering in his left hand and incense in a box in his right. In Greek fashion his hair is short, secured by a laurel wreath, and he stands with his left leg advanced. He is dressed in Greek costume, a chiton (short-sleeved tunic) partly covered by a himation (cloak). From the sanctuary of Apollo at Idalion, c.475-450 BC. Height 98 cm (38.6 in).*

54 Left *Upper part of a colossal limestone statue of a bearded man, perhaps a worshipper or a priest of Apollo. He is dressed in Greek fashion in a chiton (short-sleeved tunic) and a himation (cloak). From the sanctuary of Apollo at Idalion, 500-480 BC. Height 104 cm (41 in).*

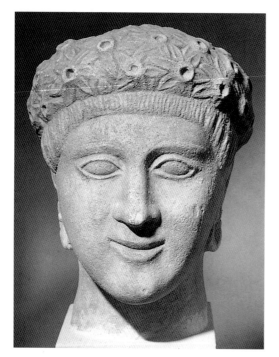

56 *Limestone head from a statue of a worshipper made by a sculptor who closely copied work of his famous Greek (Athenian) contemporaries such as Pheidias and Polycleitus. From the sanctuary of Apollo at Idalion, 450-400 BC. Height 18 cm (7.1 in).*

artificially curled, and short hair curled over the forehead and secured by a wreath. Slowly this style stagnated, and the later examples are very poorly carved. Alongside these are pieces which reflect the Classical style [56] that had been developed in mainland Greece. They were perhaps partly inspired by imported works such as the bronze head from Tamassos known as the 'Chatsworth Apollo' after its previous home. Nearly all small terracotta figurines were now made in moulds and some of the moulds themselves may have been imported from Greece. Greek dress is the norm, as are classical features. Maidens of Greek type sit on the shoulders of vessels, pouring from a small jug (see fig. 43). A series of horsemen is more readily identifiable as Cypriot. These keep their prominent noses and varied headdresses.

Cypriot sculptures of the Hellenistic and Roman periods in general reflect the styles which were fairly universal throughout the Greek-dominated eastern Mediterranean. Until the first century BC the Cypriot characteristics survived to some extent, since the principal medium remained the local 'limestone', and many of the statues continued to be dedicated in sanctuaries rather than acting as memorials or decorating public buildings, as was the case elsewhere. Following the canon ascribed by the Roman author Pliny in the first century AD to the Greek sculptor Lysippos of Sikyon (active *c*.370/360-305 BC), the heads were smaller and the bodies more slender and tightly knit, so that the statues appeared taller. Portraits became more fashionable and many representations of worshippers appear to have their facial features based on those of their Ptolemaic rulers (see fig. 12). Heads are normally fairly round and fleshy. Many men have their hair short and bound by a wreath, but some wear it long, arranged in corkscrew curls. The women's longer hair is often put up into a bun at the back, and a modified version of the *chiton*, now girded just below the breasts, became a favourite dress. The men's tunic is often only knee-length, while the cloak may be wrapped around the waist and then drawn up over the shoulder and partly across the body. Oriental figures wear Persian peaked caps made of soft material. Virtually all terracotta figurines were cast in moulds. Some, following the tradition of Alexandria in Egypt, were covered after firing by a thick lime wash on which the paint was applied. Most of the types and motifs conform to general Hellenistic taste inspired by mainland Greece, with the eastern influence mainly forgotten. Loose inexpressive forms are concealed by over-elaborate drapery, a *chiton* and *himation* for the women, a large cloak for the men. The finest examples belong to the 'Tanagra' group [57], which takes its name from the site in Boeotia in northern Greece where such pieces were first found, although it is now clear that the style developed in Athens, whence it spread to all corners of the Hellenistic world. Both men and women have small heads and lean bodies and are tightly draped. The women typically have their hair arranged in the 'melon coiffure', divided on the crown into segments and combed into a bun at the back.

57 Left *Two terracotta figurines of the 'Tanagra' class, a man and a woman tightly draped with small heads and lean bodies. Both from Amathus and probably made in Cyprus in the 3rd century* BC. *Height of woman 21 cm (8.3 in).*

The sculpture of Roman Cyprus comprises a typical mixture of large draped statues, portraits of the different emperors and copies of Greek originals. Statues of rulers and gods were now erected everywhere and adorned public buildings. The tradition of working in 'limestone' continued, and in this medium were draped statues in the traditional *chiton* with the *himation* now forming a roll around the waist and falling almost vertically down from the shoulder (see fig. 79). The later examples (*c.*AD 130-50) show much use of the drill and polishing of smooth surfaces in imitation of marble statues. Marble had indeed become much more common. The material must have been imported, but it remains uncertain whether the finished products were carved locally by skilled Cypriots or itinerant sculptors, or else arrived ready-made from the major sculpture workshops in Asia Minor or Greece. A woman's head from Salamis of the second century AD [58] has the heavy facial proportions typical of that era. After AD 250 the Hellenistic realistic tradition broke down, and this resulted in less rational representations of the anatomy and sometimes more expressive gestures. Very little sculpture dating from this time has been found in Cyprus.

58 Above *Marble portrait head from a statue of a woman. Found in the gymnasium at Salamis, 2nd century* AD. *Height 23 cm (9 in).*

Chapter Seven | Jewellery

THE ANCIENT CYPRIOTS delighted in sumptuous jewellery. In the fourth century BC their kings gained a reputation for soft living and ostentatious displays of wealth, including the use of purple fabrics: flax was an important crop. Salamis was the home of Akesas and his son Helikon, who were considered the foremost weavers of their day. A certain Hebdomaios describes himself as a fisher of murex shellfish (which would have provided the purple dye) on a monument set up to his mother at Marion around 300 BC. Jewellery was worn by the first inhabitants on the island, and from early times representations of human figures were adorned with elaborate ornaments.

Most of the raw materials for jewellery came from the east. Gold became plentiful in the Late Bronze Age, when Egypt and Syria were the principal sources. Following Alexander's conquest of the Persian Empire in the fourth century BC, gold again became widely available in the eastern Mediterranean. Asia Minor (modern Turkey) was a major supplier of silver to the ancient world. Cyprus may also have obtained some from mainland Greek mines, particularly in the fifth century BC when the exceptionally rich vein at Laurion in Attica was discovered and intensively worked.

Precious raw materials reached the craftsmen as coins or 'dumps' (blocks). Most dumps were fashioned either into sheet metal by ham-

59 *Jewellery of the Late Bronze Age from Cyprus:* a) *a pair of gold earrings, the wire hoops threaded with bulls' heads;* b) *a pair of gold earrings in the form of tapered hoops;* c) *a pair of gold earrings with clusters of beads (the 'mulberry' type);* d) *a gold pendant in the form of a pomegranate;* e) *a necklace of beads of cornelian and gold, including sixteen in the form of double shields. Length of necklace 35 cm (13.8 in).*

mering over an anvil or into wire, normally by hammering out, or occasionally by twisting a strip cut from the block and rolling it between plates until it reached the required thickness. Charcoal fires provided the heat needed for processes such as soldering (joining pieces together by melting), annealing (strengthening by exposure to heat) and casting in moulds. Sheet metal was often embossed: either in the repoussé technique when patterns were formed freehand by hammering from the back (see fig. 2), or by stamping, a technique that enabled a pattern to be repeated with the aid of specially made punches applied to the front or the back. Forms were reproduced by working sheet metal into moulds of bronze, terracotta or wood, or over a removable core. Straps and chains, which played a vital role in jewellery-making, were formed of wire. Granulation (attaching grains of precious metals to the surface) [59d, 60] and filigree (applying wire) [61] were among the principal decorative processes. Patterns could be chased (a process by which metal was displaced) or engraved (when metal was actually removed). Gold or silver plating was achieved by pressing foil over a core of some other material. In gilding [62c], gold leaf was normally attached by adhesive, though mercury gilding (mixing gold and mercury to form a spreadable paste-like amalgam from which the mercury vaporises when heated, leaving a gold layer), introduced

60 Above *Gold finger-ring with cloisonné enamel decoration surrounded by two rows of granulation on the bezel. From a tomb at (Old) Paphos, 1200-1150 BC. Depth 2.2 cm (0.9 in).*

61 Right *Pair of gold-plated bronze spiral earrings, ending in horned griffin heads with enamel and filigree decoration. This type of earring was a Cypriot speciality and this particular material favoured by Cypriot jewellers. From Amathus, 425-400 BC. Length 3.5 cm (1.4 in).*

62 Right *Hellenistic and Roman finger-rings from Cyprus:* a) (top right) *a gold ring-setting with sunken relief decoration showing the sanctuary of Aphrodite at (Old) Paphos, 2nd-3rd century AD;* b) (top left) *the same scene and the goddess Isis engraved on a gold ring with a double bezel, 2nd-3rd century AD;* c) (bottom left) *a gilded bronze ring with a glass setting, late 4th century BC;* d) (bottom right) *a gold ring with two sapphire settings, 3rd-4th century AD. Depth of sapphire ring 2.3 cm (0.9 in).*

63 *Jewellery of the Roman period from Cyprus dating to the 2nd or 3rd century AD:* a) *a pair of gold earrings with glass settings;* b) *two gold earrings (not a pair) with pendants;* c) *a gold necklace with garnet beads and a wheel motif with garnet settings in the centre. Length of necklace 33 cm (13 in).*

some time in the Hellenistic period, became popular in Roman times. The addition of enamel (coloured glass fused to a metallic base) and the inlay of coloured stones and glass [63] gave a polychrome effect.

The early communities wore necklaces of locally available dentalium shells and beads of cornelian that came from the east (see p. 37). In the Chalcolithic period picrolite (a soft soap-like stone) was used to make pendants. These were often in the form of human figures shaped like a cross similar to many of the larger figurines in the same material (see fig. 8). Groups of dentalium shells were still used for necklaces. An important innovation around 2500 BC was the use of seals of stone apparently to stamp pottery or personal items. This was a short-lived practice not revived until about a thousand years later.

Copper and rarely gold were very occasionally used for jewellery from shortly before 2000 BC. A century later faience (glazed powdered quartz) was imported from Egypt to make beads. As we have already seen (p. 31), bronze dress-pins now became quite widely used.

It was in the Late Bronze Age that gold became common, imported from the east along with most other raw materials. The east, Egypt and Mycenaean Greece provided some finished products but more often introduced techniques, types and decorative motifs, which were adopted and adapted by Cypriot artisans. Granulation was learnt from Mycenaean Greece, but Cypriot innovations probably included the loop-in-loop chain and the use of gold wire, either as applied decoration or to form beads and rings. In form dress-pins and funerary diadems and mouth-pieces (see fig. 2) are eastern, but the stamped decoration on the funerary pieces is often of Mycenaean Greek inspiration, while several of the pins incorporate the Cypriot loop-in-loop chain [64]. The finger-rings with decorated bezels have the bezel in line with the hoop in Egyptian fashion (in Mycenaean Greece and Minoan Crete the bezel was set at right angles to the hoop), but the decorative motifs are Mycenaean or pe-culiarly Cypriot. The swivel finger-ring was another Egyptian invention, although it probably reached Cyprus by way of Syria and Palestine, while finger-rings with circular bezels filled with coloured glass are a Mycenaean Greek type. Particularly popu-lar in Cyprus and probably a local invention were earrings with pendants in the form of bulls' heads [59a], though other styles of earrings such as the tapered hoop [59b] and 'mulberry' (decorated with a cluster of beads) [59c] were of eastern origin. First made in Cyprus about 1400 BC, the latter types remained popular right until the Archaic period. Necklaces made up of beads of mixed foreign and local origin [59e] illustrate the amalgam of influences in Late Bronze Age Cyprus.

A long version of the tapered hoop, which was more or less leech-shaped and adapted from a Syrian design, was worn in the twelfth century. Also new at this time, and indeed unknown before in the Bronze Age Greek world, was true cloisonné enam-elling. This process involved forming cloisons (cells) by solder-ing thin strips of metal to the background and filling them with enamel. This technique is used for the decoration of the bezels of gold rings [60], which in other respects are similar to those with circular bezels inlaid simply with coloured glass. To the eleventh century BC belong gold versions of the D-shaped *fibula*, originally introduced from the Bronze Age Greek world. Another innovation was the manufacture of gold plaques of eastern design, which would have formed tiara-like head-dresses (*poloi*), and other plaques were simply decorated with rosettes. These jewellery designs continued throughout the next three centuries.

In the Archaic period (750-475 BC) the jewellery for the most part continued the types that were now well established in the Cypriot reper-toire, although techniques improved and the decoration was more elab-orate, often enriched with fine granulation. Connections were estab-lished with artisans in the Greek east: in the seventh century BC Cyprus introduced the gold-embossed plaques to Rhodes, and common both in Cyprus and at Ephesus were earrings with 'boat-shaped' hollow hoops to which the pins were attached. These earrings were of Syrian origin, but it is not clear whether the Cypriot examples were made locally or

64 *Two gold dress-pins with ornamental heads. The upper part of the shank of the right-hand example, topped by a faience bead, is formed from a double loop-in-loop chain, a western Asiatic type modified by Cypriot jewellers. From Enkomi, c.14th century BC. Length of longest 13.2 cm (5.2 in).*

imported from East Greece. Also in the seventh century BC other types of earrings, the tapered hoop and the 'mulberry' which had survived in Cyprus through the 'Dark Age', were re-introduced to the Greek world.

A new series of gems, which were often set in rings and used like sealstones to impress the owner's mark on documents and possessions, began in the Greek world around 580 BC. These were made of hard stones in the form of an Egyptian scarab beetle, and the decoration was engraved with a drill and a wheel [65]. This art was learnt by the Greeks from the Phoenicians, probably in Cyprus, where the two communities lived side by side. The many gems of the later sixth and earlier fifth centuries found in Cyprus, several of which bear Cypriot inscriptions, suggest that the Greek Cypriot workshops continued in existence, although their products in both their subject matter and style are similar to those from Greek island and Ionian (East Greek) workshops. The Semon Master, who was active between about 500 and 480 BC and was one of the two major artists of the late Archaic period, may have worked in Cyprus.

Filigree became more popular than granulation in the Classical period and enamel, bordered by filigree, was used for inlay. Silver became common (perhaps now obtained from Greece), but gold-plated bronze was the medium favoured by Cypriot jewellers. Popular in Cyprus and probably made locally were bracelets with open ends terminating in animal heads, and others in the form of

65 *Two gems from Cyprus:* (left) *a plasma scaraboid by the Semon Master showing a youth drawing his bow accompanied by his dog, 500-480 BC;* (right) *the back of a cornelian gem, in the form of a scarab beetle, from Amathus, 550-500 BC.*

snakes, though both of these varieties were known earlier in the Greek world. Other favourite types probably made locally included spiral rings; whether for the ears or hair, they often terminate in female or animal heads that are worked in repoussé and attached to the spiral by collars with filigree ornament that sometimes outline enamel inlays [61]. Quite common were gold pendants in the form of vases or acorns, the latter sometimes made of cornelian with a gold cap. Some fine jewellery was imported from the Greek world, such as an intricate pair of gold earrings in the form of inverted pyramids surmounted by birds and rosettes which were probably made in one of the East Greek cities on the west coast of Asia Minor (modern Turkey).

Personal jewellery was plentiful in Hellenistic and Roman Cyprus, although since Cypriot artisans followed cosmopolitan fashions it is often unclear whether individual items were made locally or imported. Techniques were generally unelaborate, and both filigree and granulation became rare. A new polychrome style was achieved by the addition of coloured stones and glass.

In the Hellenistic period (325-30 BC) some finger-rings became mounts for engraved or precious stones or glass set in large bezels [62c]. They indicated the official status of the owner. Snake finger-rings were common throughout the eastern Mediterranean, but Cyprus imported its glass finger-rings from Syrian workshops. Earrings of twisted wire, sometimes threaded with coloured beads and with elaborate terminals [66b], were perhaps a Cypriot creation. A new motif, the 'Herakles knot' [66c], was adopted throughout the Hellenistic world from Egypt. Eros was a favourite motif on the island [66a]. Much of the jewellery found in Cyprus at this time, such as chain necklaces terminating in a Herakles knot or animal heads and earrings with pendants, are also common elsewhere.

Hellenistic traditions continued into the early Roman period and the ostentatious finger-rings now signified the military status of the wearer. A change came about after the second century AD with the introduction of the piercing of gold in a kind of network technique and the

66 *Gold jewellery of the late Classical and Hellenistic periods from Cyprus dating from the mid-4th and 3rd centuries* BC: a) *a pendant from a necklace with two figures of Eros perching on a myrtle flower;* b) *a pair of earrings of twisted wire terminating in lions' heads;* c) *a chain necklace with a lion's head at each end; one of the lions holds a 'Herakles' (reef) knot in its mouth. Length of necklace 31.3 cm (12.3 in).*

more abundant use of coloured stones. Many rather plain types of earrings were produced [63a,b]. Necklaces of chains or straps now often incorporated the popular wheel motif [63c], but others were more simply composed of gold links with semi-precious stones or glass beads. Of local manufacture were the finger-rings with engraved and sunken relief decoration on the bezels sold as souvenirs to pilgrims visiting the sanctuary of Aphrodite at (Old) Paphos [62a,b]. It is clear, therefore, that Cypriot jewellers remained active even into late antiquity and continued to manufacture at least some truly 'Cypriot' items.

Chapter Eight | Religion and burial customs

67 *Red Polished plank-shaped figurine cradling a child; a fertility charm. 19th-18th century* BC. *Height 26 cm (10.2 in).*

To RECREATE the religious beliefs and practices of a past civilisation is notoriously difficult. The lack of documentary evidence in the form of inscribed representations naming the deity or descriptive texts makes the task even harder. Burial customs are easier to unravel. Tombstones and sarcophagi (coffins) and, more importantly, many of the actual graves survive, still containing the goods given to the dead to accompany them to the next world. These grave gifts are sometimes the principal evidence for the material culture of a particular period.

Religious beliefs and practices

The beliefs of prehistoric Cyprus remain obscure, but the concept of fertility was evidently paramount. Whether the early human figurines of the stump and cruciform varieties (see p. 48) are to be identified as fertility charms or fertility goddesses [67], in practical terms their function would have been the same. These religious beliefs continued even though in the Late Bronze Age (1650-1050 BC) greater foreign influence is apparent in both representations and practice. The new Syrian type of female figurine is often described as the 'Astarte' type (see fig. 49 right), taking the name of the eastern mother goddess. However, as this identification of such figurines found in their homeland is far from certain, doubt must also remain over the assumption that the Cypriot examples are goddesses.

The earliest sanctuary remains are of this period. The first were built in the later fifteenth century BC. The major period of construction was around 1200 BC (see fig. 15), while worship continued in some of the earlier foundations into the twelfth century. Most were close to settlements, and some to copper workshops. Several represent a Near Eastern type of court sanctuary consisting of a walled *temenos* (open court), with a small covered 'holy of holies' or other cult buildings. The altar, often crowned by handmade bulls' horns, known as 'horns of consecration', usually stood in the open air. Worship occasionally took place in rooms within larger structures.

Some idea of the religious customs can be gained from the objects discovered in these sanctuaries. Practices such as the wearing of anthropomorphic masks and the offering of models of kidneys apparently used in divination reflect customs known earlier in Syria and Palestine. Among the dedications were small copper ingots and remarkable bronze statuettes. The last included a horned male figure [69] and a female 'Astarte', with her hands held at her breasts, both standing on ingots. They must represent protectors, perhaps divine, of the copper industry. In the sanctuaries of these 'horned gods' quantities of horned animals were sacrificed and animal masks were apparently worn. Both here and elsewhere libations were offered.

The typical sanctuary of the earlier Iron Age combined a walled *temenos* with small cult buildings and altars. The larger cities had several shrines, nearly all situated away from the settlements to which they belonged, although the sacred precincts of the Phoenician Astarte at Kition-Kathari and of Aphrodite-Astarte and Cybele at Tamassos were close to copper workshops. Soloi and the neighbouring town of Paradisotissa had small temples on the Greek plan with *pronaos* (porch or vestibule) and *cella* (principal hall) but these were very rare in Cyprus until a much later date.

Although there is some documentary evidence for the gods worshipped in Archaic and Classical Cyprus (750-325 BC), very few of the surviving representations are actually named, so the identification of individual statues of gods and goddesses remains problematical.

The principal deity was the Great Mother Goddess. She was identified above all with Aphrodite, the Cypriot goddess par excellence, who was already described as 'the Cyprian' in the eighth-century BC poems of Homer and the slightly later works of Hesiod. Her sanctuary at (Old) Paphos was the chief religious centre of the island and famous throughout the ancient Mediterranean world. The early Greek writers call her Aphrodite, while dedications in other sanctuaries in Cyprus in the sixth century BC name her simply 'the Paphian'. At (Old) Paphos itself the first dedicatory inscriptions are of the fourth century BC. In these she is simply called 'Wanassa', the 'lady'. This is a very old title, perhaps known already in Linear B texts from Mycenaean Greece. It apparently signifies the great antiquity of the cult. At (Old) Paphos too she was represented by a conical stone [68], obviously a symbol of fertility as in many other oriental and Mediterranean

68 *Part of the sanctuary of Aphrodite at (Old) Paphos on a bronze coin of Cyprus issued under the Roman emperor Caracalla (AD 198-217). Her dove feeds in the courtyard in front of the building, and there are more doves on the roof. The cult image, in the central tower, is a conical stone.*

69 Above *Bronze statuette representing the protector, perhaps divine, of the copper industry. He wears a horned helmet, carries a shield and spear and stands on an ingot shaped like an oxhide. From the 'sanctuary of the ingot god' at Enkomi. 12th century BC. Height 35 cm (13.8 in).*

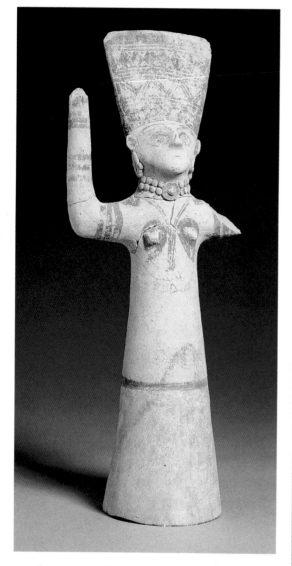

cults. This aniconic worship of Aphrodite was, however, peculiar to Paphos. Among the offerings made in the sanctuary in the Archaic period are many terracotta figurines of women wearing tall hats and with their arms upraised [70]. These may represent either the goddess herself or her worshippers. If they are indeed representations of the goddess offered by worshippers, there would be reason to identify all the Cypriot representations of women in tall hats or crowns as Aphrodite. Raising the arms is a well-known gesture of worship, but some scholars argue for the introduction of a cult of a 'goddess with uplifted arms' from Crete in the eleventh century BC. The true answer to these questions may never be known. However, whatever interpretation is given to the many female figures from sanctuaries, it is clear that the worship of a fertility goddess remained supreme in Cyprus.

Cypriot gods included a principal male deity and various local gods, including one of the woodland (Hylates) and another of music, perhaps the deified Kinyras, the legendary founder and first king of Paphos.

The Phoenicians introduced their own deities. Of their pantheon, there is documentary evidence in Cyprus for the worship of the goddesses Astarte and Anat, and the gods Baal, Eshmoun, Reshef, Mikal, Melqart and Shed. Egyptian cults of 'Bes', Ptah, Hathor and Thoeris were introduced by the Phoenicians early in the Archaic period, before the time of Egyptian rule. Small represen-

70 *Above Painted terracotta figurine of a woman with her arms upraised, bedecked with jewellery and wearing a polos (tall hat): a worshipper or a fertility goddess, perhaps Aphrodite herself. From a tomb near (Old) Paphos, 7th century BC. Height 36 cm (14.2 in).*

71 *Terracotta figurines of the Egyptian dwarf gods 'Bes', bearded and with leonine features, and Ptah. Their cults were introduced to Cyprus by the Phoenicians. Both were made in the 6th century BC and were found at Amathus. Height of 'Bes' 17 cm (6.7 in).*

tations of these particular deities were often made into charms to ward off evil [71]. From about 500 BC Hathor may have been identified with Aphrodite (see fig. 17). Phoenician dedications in the sanctuary at (Old) Paphos, destroyed by the Persians for their siege mound (see p. 87), included votive monuments similar to those found in their sanctuaries in the western Mediterranean world. Egyptian influence in the years of Egyptian domination includes a single dedication to Isis on a bronze jug offered 'to the god' at Kourion and the invention by Cypriot sculptors of representations of the god Ammon, known to the Greeks as Zeus Ammon. The first examples show a ram-headed god on a throne supported by rams, while the type with a human head, popular in Cyprus from 550/525 BC, is similar to, and may have inspired, a version found on coins of 520-480 BC of Cyrene in Libya.

There is difficulty in naming anonymous representations of some of these deities. Popular dedications in sanctuaries of Astarte in both Phoenicia and Cyprus were terracotta figurines of pregnant women, which at least confirm her role as a fertility goddess. It is uncertain by what name the Cypriots knew statues of a male figure dressed in a tunic covered by a lionskin, brandishing a club in one hand and holding a lion in the other. The representations, most of which are of the fifth and fourth centuries BC, are reminiscent of both the Phoenician Melqart and the Greek Herakles [72].

There is no firm evidence that the worship of Greek deities was established in Cyprus before the fourth century BC, with the exception of fifth-century cults of Athena at Idalion and Vouni. The cult of Zeus at Salamis had a reputation for great antiquity. Literary texts of the Roman period claim that it dates from the foundation of the city in the eleventh century BC. In this they echo a comment by an Athenian orator writing around 374-365 BC, which confirms its existence in the fourth century but not necessarily earlier. A 'great god' was certainly worshipped at Salamis from an early date, but whether he was known as Zeus equally early remains uncertain.

It was therefore in the fourth century BC that Greek cults became widespread in the island. At this time too Cypriot and Phoenician gods and goddesses started to become identified with Greek deities. The principal god may henceforth have been known as Zeus, at least at Salamis. The Cypriot Hylates and the Phoenician Reshef both became identified with the Greek Apollo. There were many local cults of Apollo in Cyprus. At Tamassos there is mention in an inscription of the fourth century BC of Apollo Alasiotas, Apollo of Alasia. While it is tempting to see this as evidence of an ancient cult of a 'god of Alasia', which would help to confirm the identification of Cyprus with Alasia, the Alashiya or Asy of the Near Eastern texts (see pp. 31-2), it is possible that the epithet Alasiotas refers to another foreign deity, although no

72 *Limestone statuette wearing a lionskin and holding a lion in his left hand. His right arm was originally upraised and held a club at his forehead. Reminiscent of both the Phoenician god Melqart and the Greek hero Herakles, the name by which he was known in Cyprus is unknown. From the sanctuary of Apollo at Idalion, 5th century BC. Height 60 cm (23.6 in).*

73 *Terracotta group of figurines of worshippers or priests putting on bull's masks in preparation for a religious ceremony. There were originally five figures in the group, but only two are preserved. From the sanctuary of Apollo at Kourion (Curium), 650-600 BC. Height 9.7 cm (3.8 in).*

dedications to him (or her) have yet been recorded outside the island. At Pyla in the Hellenistic period there was an Apollo Keraeatas, Apollo of the horns, but it is difficult to see in this a reflection of a Late Bronze Age cult of horned gods, which itself is not assured. Also in the fourth century BC the Cypriot Aphrodite became identified with the Phoenician Astarte (although at (Old) Paphos this did not happen until the third century BC) and Anat, and with the Greek Athena as well. Anat was also identified with the Greek Athena, while at Kition the cult of the Phoenician Eshmoun became the cult of the Greek Asklepios. The Greek huntress goddess, Artemis, was also worshipped and the Kitians established a cult of their own, Artemis Paralia (Artemis of the sea-coast). In their final years in the late fourth century BC some of the kings of the cities made strenuous efforts to Hellenise their kingdoms, and in so doing propagated Greek cults. Dedications were now made for the first time to Hera and also to Demeter and Kore (see fig. 88).

In the Archaic and Classical periods the sanctuaries were hives of activity. Here the gods were believed to reside and even participate in the sacred banquets accompanied by ritual dancing celebrated in their honour. The priests wore animal and anthropomorphic masks [73], animals (and occasionally humans) were sacrificed, libations were offered and incense burnt. The offerings included many statues and statuettes of limestone and terracotta (and occasionally of bronze) which the devotees believed acted as substitutes for themselves as continuous worshippers. Some idea of the identity of the deity may be gained from the dedications; in the sanctuaries of gods statuettes of horsemen and chariots are common while in those of the fertility goddess bearers of offerings, mostly women, worshippers (or the goddess herself) with upraised arms and musicians [74] predominate. Locks of hair were offered to the Phoenician goddess Astarte. Sacred prostitution in the cults of Aphrodite at (Old) Paphos and of Astarte at Kition is recorded in certain texts. At Kition it is said to have involved women and young boys. This may provide an explanation for the dedication of statues of small boys ('temple boys') [75] which continued into the Hellenistic period. A pair of terracotta statuettes of boys completely naked were dedicated to

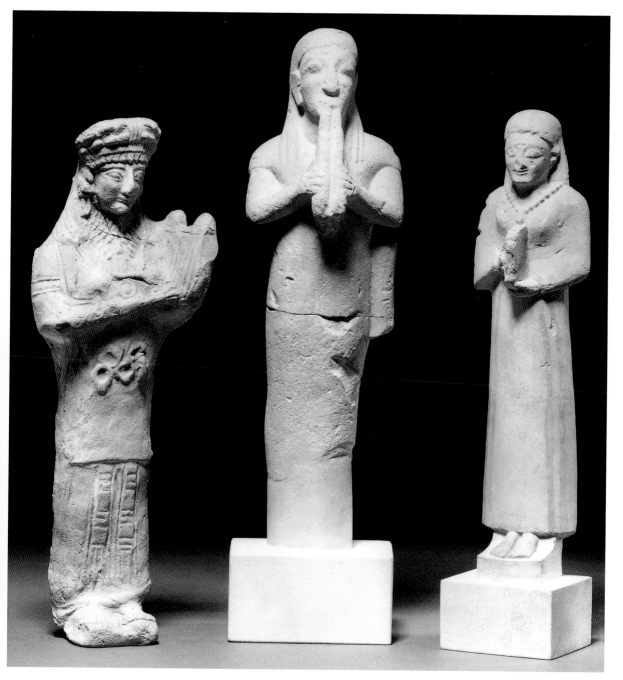

74 *Group of musicians representing participants in a religious ceremony accompanying sacred dances:* a) *a terracotta female lyre-player bedecked with jewellery and wearing a tunic with a sash, from Achna;* b) *a limestone figure playing pipes, from Tamassos;* c) *a limestone female tambourine-player wearing a long tunic decorated with red painted stripes, from Amathus. 6th century* BC. *Height of lyre-player 39 cm (15.3 in).*

75 *Limestone statue of a crouching child wearing rich jewellery and holding a rabbit beside him in his left hand. Commonly known as 'temple boys', these statues were often dedicated in sanctuaries in Cyprus. They may represent temple servants or prostitutes, or simply commemorate the occasion when a boy made his first offering in the sanctuary. From the sanctuary of Apollo at Idalion, c.300 BC. Height 41 cm (16.1 in).*

Eshmoun in his sanctuary near Sidon (Phoenicia) around 330 BC. This suggests that sacred prostitution was another Phoenician or oriental trait in Cypriot religion. A 'master of the water' is described as presiding over the dispensing of libations at Kition.

Cyprus's religious institutions were naturally affected by Ptolemaic rule. From the early second century BC the *strategos* received the title of High Priest, which enabled him to collect the revenues from all the sanctuaries and so enrich the royal coffers. The worship of the ruling Ptolemy, the Dynastic cult, became of prime importance. A special organisation known as the 'Koinon [confederation] of Cypriots' was set up to promote it. However, existing religious practices were scarcely interfered with and worship continued at many of the traditional open sanctuaries and rustic shrines. In the third century BC many dedications were made to a nymph in a remote hilltop shrine at Kaphizin (near

Nicosia), where she may already have been worshipped for many centuries. Being Greeks themselves, the Ptolemies promoted Greek cults. Greek deities worshipped included Zeus, Apollo, Dionysos, Pan or Melanthios, Poseidon, Asklepios (and Hygeia), Athena, Hera and Artemis. Aphrodite remained the supreme goddess, now more often identified with Astarte, whose cult survived. Frequently identified with Aphrodite was Arsinoe, the wife of Ptolemy II Philadelphus (285-245 BC), deified on her death in 270 BC. Her cult enjoyed particular popularity in Cyprus and may well have started during her lifetime. Cities were founded in her name, including one on the former site of Marion, which had been destroyed in 312 BC. The Ptolemies also introduced cults of Egyptian deities, including Serapis and Isis. Some Egyptian gods were equated with Greek deities, as Zeus was with the Libyan Ammon.

Dedications continued in many of the open sanctuaries. Some were constructed, such as those to Aphrodite and Serapis and Isis near Soloi, and others were rebuilt, as was the sanctuary of Astarte-Aphrodite and Cybele at Tamassos. Inscriptions record the construction of temples in the cities, but their remains seldom survive. Exceptions are the temple of Zeus at Salamis, a temple on the acropolis at Soloi and one on the Fanari hill at (New) Paphos, all of the Greek type. The Salamis temple was built on a podium in the second century BC and that at (New) Paphos was constructed on a stepped platform at about the same time.

Having worshipped their Ptolemaic rulers, the Cypriots found no difficulty in transferring their loyalty to the Roman emperors. The Imperial cult was as important as the Dynastic cult had been. The Koinon became an officially recognised central organisation. Its headquarters were at the sanctuary of Aphrodite at (Old) Paphos which was now joined by a sacred way to the new city. One of its principal functions was to promote the worship of the Roman emperors. Some of the traditional rites survived, as did the worship of Greek deities. The cult of the Paphian Aphrodite remained pre-eminent [68]. Musical and literary contests were among the popular ceremonies at her annual feast. As in the Hellenistic period, there are many more temples recorded in inscriptions than actually survive. The temple of Zeus at Salamis was rebuilt. Traditional sanctuaries were remodelled and enlarged, but the earlier cult place was always included in the new design. At Curium (Kourion) and Amathus a classic Greco-Roman temple became the focal point of the redesigned sanctuary, but at (Old) Paphos the basic Near Eastern plan remained.

Its geographical position and the presence of a strong Jewish community meant that Cyprus was one of the first areas of Christian mission. Paul and Barnabas (a native of Salamis) visited the island in AD 45. Cyprus did not, however, fully embrace Christianity until it became the official religion of the Roman Empire in the late fourth century AD.

Burial customs

Inhumation was the normal funerary rite in ancient Cyprus. Cremation occurred only rarely, as a result of foreign contact. The first settlers

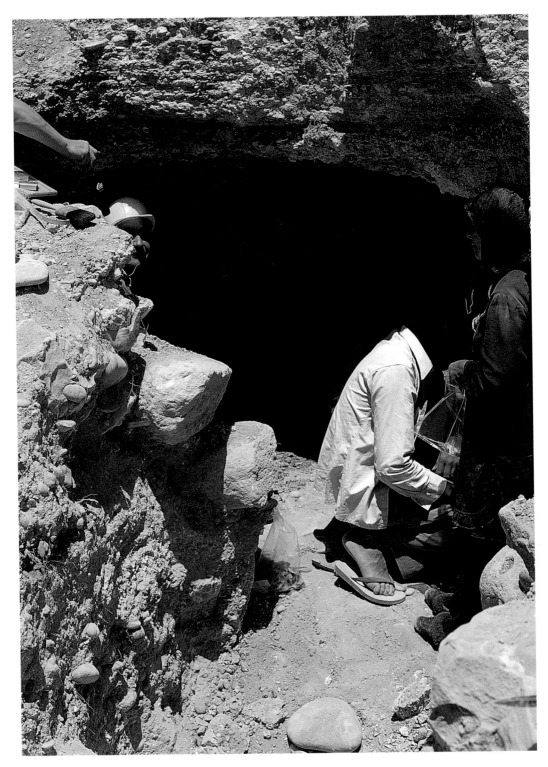

76 *A typical rock-cut chamber tomb approached by a dromos (entrance passage) of the early Archaic period, in the Xylinos cemetery at (Old) Paphos.*

buried their dead under the floors of their houses or in pits outside. Pit graves continued to be the usual type of tomb in the Chalcolithic period (4000/3900-2500 BC), although there was now more variety, including the appearance of a new bottle-shaped type of deep pit in western Cyprus. Towards the end of the period the same region provides evidence of practices foreshadowing Bronze Age customs: the pit graves were now occasionally set apart from settlements in cemeteries and, even more rarely, the dead were accompanied by gifts. A few rock-cut chamber tombs are also known, but these have hitherto been found only under houses inside a settlement.

The real changes in practice occurred soon after 2500 BC. Tombs were now normally cut in the rock; the dead were buried in irregularly shaped chambers approached by short pit-like entrance passages (*dromoi*) [76]. The graves were regularly in cemeteries, away from the settlements, and the dead were accompanied by gifts. The same tomb might be used on more than one occasion. With some variations, this type of tomb and these customs were the most common throughout the Bronze Age.

Variations from the norm included the reappearance of bottle-shaped pits with no entrance passages in a cemetery in the south-west in the later third millennium. In some cemeteries of the seventeenth century BC a rather different type of tomb occurs, with a kidney-shaped chamber approached by stairs in a long, wedge-shaped passage.

At Enkomi and also at (Old) Paphos and Kalavassos-Ayios Dhimitrios in the Late Bronze Age some of the dead were again buried under the houses. Most common are the normal rock-cut chamber tombs, but at Enkomi there are some tombs of a different construction. These must have been for the wealthy or ruling class. It may be significant that the earliest (of the sixteenth century BC) has a conical roof, like an old-fashioned beehive, built of stone blocks, similar to the *tholos* tombs of Mycenaean Greece, but the others have no close parallels in the Bronze Age Greek world.

In cemeteries of the eleventh century BC rock-cut tombs of the Mycenaean Greek type, with long narrow *dromoi* and rectangular chambers, occur alongside the traditional Cypriot variety. Cremation, as in the Greek world, was practised, as well as the more usual inhumation. Together, the new type of tomb and the cremation of some of the dead help to confirm the arrival of Greek colonists in Cyprus by this time.

Rock-cut chamber tombs, with wider *dromoi* and many minor variations in overall plan, remained the normal graves for the ordinary people until the end of the Roman era. But for the aristocracy of the city-kingdoms tombs were being constructed on a larger scale. At Salamis monumental tombs, their façades crowned by Egyptian cornices, were built in the late eighth and seventh centuries BC. They had extremely wide entrance passages to accommodate the wheeled vehicles which transported the dead to burial. The vehicles were drawn by horses or donkeys, which were then sacrificed to accompany the dead to the other world. In the richest of the tombs four vehicles were discovered; the draught animals had bronze harnesses and trappings. The grave goods were exceptionally rich, including bronze vessels and furniture with ivory fittings. All these items were imported from different parts of the Near East or, if made locally, show strong eastern influence. They constitute an appropriate display of finery for a despot living on the western fringe of the Assyrian Empire. A set of thirty-three Greek vases in another tomb may be evidence for an exchange of gifts between Greek and Cypriot noble families. In other tombs cattle and, perhaps, a slave or prisoner were sacrificed and *amphorae* containing olive oil were offered. Iron spits have also been found, associated with fire-dogs, recalling the kitchen gear of heroes in the epic poems of Homer. One tomb was finally covered by a huge mound, and there are a few cases of cremation. Some scholars have seen these tombs and their customs as mirroring the burial practices described in Homer's poems. If so, they may have been inspired by the epic poetry which was circulating in the eighth century BC. Otherwise, they may simply represent a continuation of Mycenaean Greek practices, albeit after a considerable time gap. This gap has been partly filled by the discovery of a heroic burial of the mid-tenth century BC at Lefkandi in Euboea.

Fine stone-built tombs of the late eighth to early fifth centuries BC have been discovered at the sites of other city-kingdoms, including Tamassos, Idalion, Kition, Amathus, Soloi and Kourion. A few occur elsewhere, as at Patriki and Trachonas. The finest are those at Tamassos, whose architecture in stone imitates wooden construction. Certain details are of Phoenician origin (see p. 20). The *dromos* of a simple rock-cut chamber tomb in the same cemetery contained the remains of horses that had been sacrificed, their bronze trappings and a bronze helmet recalling the practices at Salamis.

For the cult of the dead evidence comes from another cemetery at Salamis, which was in use from around 700 to 300 BC. Pyres were discovered close by or actually in the *dromoi* of simple rock-cut tombs. In the ashes were a number of offerings, all burnt, including vases evidently smashed after a libation had been offered. A similar custom was practised in Athens, but there the pyres were associated with cremation. In the same cemetery at Salamis children were buried in vessels, either

77 Limestone sarcophagus, a Cypriot version of an originally Phoenician type of mummy-shaped sarcophagus. The box is rounded at the top and is provided with feet in the Cypriot tradition. On the lid is the head of a bearded man, presumably the occupant. From a tomb at Amathus, c.450 BC. Length 190 cm (74.8 in).

Phoenician jars or *amphorae* of Cypriot or Greek manufacture. This was a very ancient burial rite, which may have been adopted by the Cypriots from Phoenicia, since only Phoenician jars were used for the burial of children in the town of Salamis between the eleventh and eighth centuries BC. Phoenician jars were also among cremation urns of the eighth century found together with evidence of libations in a cemetery at Amathus.

On the outskirts of another cemetery at Salamis a short rock-cut *dromos* leads to a burial chamber with a vaulted roof and paved floor. The whole of the interior of the chamber carries painted decoration exactly like the inside of an Egyptian sarcophagus. Belonging to the middle years of the sixth century BC, this is evidence of direct influence from Egypt during the period of Egyptian rule.

In the Classical period burial customs changed little, although sarcophagi, known only rarely earlier, became more common. Simple versions, carved from solid blocks or made of slabs fitted together, were used in ordinary graves. More elaborate examples with fine relief decoration (see fig. 95) were made for aristocrats or kings early in the period, and later marble mummy-shaped coffins were imported from Phoenicia. Phoenicians at Kition made their own mummy-shaped sarcophagi locally. A Cypriot-made example from Amathus shows only the head, and keeps specifically Cypriot features [77]. From this period too graves were more often marked by tombstones or statues. Towards the end of the fourth century tomb chambers tended to become more rectangular with niches in the sides and with entrances lined with masonry looking forward to Hellenistic tomb architecture. A particularly large tomb of this type in the vicinity of (Old) Paphos was originally built for two mid-

78 *View of the courtyard of one of the subterranean 'tombs of the Kings' carved in the rock for the aristocrats or ruling class at (New) Paphos in the Hellenistic period. They mirror those in cemeteries in the newly founded city of Alexandria in Egypt.*

fourth-century kings. Ptolemaic and Roman rule had little effect on established practices, except that niches and *loculi* (larger rectangular extensions) were regularly cut into some chamber tombs to enlarge the accommodation for the dead and their gifts, and the entrance passages were lined with masonry. Some of the dead were buried in simple shafts or pits. Rock-cut subterranean tombs in Hellenistic Paphos are versions of those found at Alexandria in Egypt [78], and must have served the aristocrats or local rulers. Some rock-cut tombs have painted chambers, recalling the sixth-century BC tomb at Salamis, and are another indication of Alexandrian customs. At Amathus gravestones bear painted decoration [79]. These may again reflect Alexandrian influence, although similar gravestones are also found in northern Greece. Tombstones [80] were generally quite common in the Hellenistic and Roman periods, as were sarcophagi.

Under the Romans in south and central Cyprus cylindrical altar-like *cippi* (small pillars) also marked the graves of the ruling and middle classes. These *cippi* had inscriptions on their shafts, which usually read simply: 'Dear ..., child of ..., fare thee well'. The wealthy were still buried in stone-built tombs. Some were newly constructed but others, including certain of the 'Alexandrian' version at (New) Paphos, were reused. Roman burials were also made in some Hellenistic rock-cut chamber tombs. The use of the same tomb for more than one generation had a long history on the island, and this must be one of the reasons for the overall conservatism of the burial customs of ancient Cyprus.

79 *Limestone stele (gravestone) with painted decoration showing a boy holding a pigeon in his outstretched left hand. Similar stelae are known from Alexandria in Egypt and from northern Greece. Found on the surface above a tomb at Amathus, c.3rd century* BC. *Height 69 cm (27.2 in).*

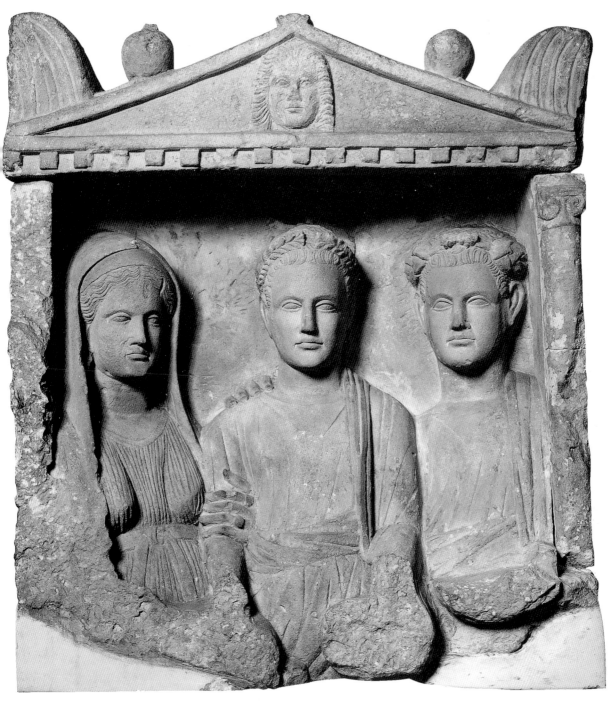

80 *Limestone grave relief showing the deceased (in the centre), probably with his mother and his brother. The men wear chitons (tunics) and himatia (cloaks), and the woman wears a chiton, girded below her breasts and partly covered by a cloak. From Tremithusa, near Golgoi, c.1st century AD. Height 98.5 cm (38.8 in).*

Chapter Nine | Coinage

COINS WERE FIRST manufactured in Cyprus in the late sixth century BC, when the island was organised into several city-kingdoms. As the rulers of these kingdoms at this time all owed allegiance and paid tribute to the Great King of Persia, it is not surprising that when the city-kingdoms began to issue coinage they all adopted the same weight standard. This weight system is known as the 'Persic' because, although it had originated not in Persia but in western Asia Minor (modern Turkey), it was taken over by the Persian conquerors of that region and eventually spread to many parts of the Persian Empire. Despite their use of the same weight system, the coins of the Cypriot city-kingdoms in the Persian period (until 330 BC) varied considerably in choice of designs, artistic style and, because of the mixed origins of the island's population, scripts: Cypriot, Phoenician and Greek.

The earliest Cypriot coins were all made of silver. They were produced by hammering an ingot of metal between two dies; the designs engraved into the dies were thus transferred to the coin. This method of minting is known as striking. At first only the lower die was engraved, but soon the upper 'punch' die was also given a recognisable design. The designs were intended to identify the authority behind the issue of coinage by way of an appropriate pictorial design, sometimes supplemented by an inscription, which would usually appear in abbreviated form. The designs are not as intelligible to us as they would have been to the people for whom the coins were originally produced, and some of the earliest issues of Cyprus have not yet been given precise attributions [81]. The designs on some early Cypriot coins are repeated on coins produced in the Greek world. This is one of the indications that at that time there was considerable movement of silver coinage between different regions. In particular, coinage from the Aegean area moved eastwards to the Persian Empire. Indeed, much Greek coinage appears as bullion in hoards of silver in the east, and these hoards, which are mostly found in Egypt and Syria, often contain Cypriot coins.

81 *The head of an eagle and scroll decoration on a silver coin of an uncertain Cypriot city; c.505 BC.*

The main denomination for Cypriot coinage in the Persian period was the double shekel, weighing about 10.8 g (0.4 oz), but to make coinage more flexible smaller denominations were also produced. By the late fifth century BC a wide range of small-denomination silver coins were in use on the island, all accurately weighed as fractions of the shekel: thirds, sixths, twelfths, twenty-fourths, and even the tiny forty-eighths, weighing little more than a tenth of a gramme. These smaller fractions would have represented the small change of the day, for buying and selling in the market-place. The British Museum collection contains a number of these pieces from a hoard found at Idalion in 1869.

In the fifth or fourth centuries BC mints were operating in virtually all the major cities of the island: coinages have been attributed to Salamis, Paphos, Kition, Idalion, Amathus, Lapithos and Marion. It is in this period, therefore, that the most varied coinage was produced, and the designs are an important source of information for religion, art and political history. Designs were chosen which symbolised the city-kingdoms or their rulers; then, once established, the same themes tended to remain on the coinage so that it would be recognised: the ram and *ankh* sign (the Egyptian symbol of life) at Salamis [82a], the bull at Paphos [82b], the sphinx and lotus flower at Idalion, and Herakles-Melqart at Kition, the chief Phoenician city [82c]. The island's ethnic and cultural mixture is well illustrated. Coin designs are mostly in the Greek tradition, accompanied usually by Cypriot lettering at Salamis, Paphos, Idalion, Amathus and Marion, and by Phoenician lettering at Kition and Lapithos. Sometimes a cultural mixture is strikingly visible. Lapithos has coins with designs featuring Greek subjects executed in typically Greek style, alongside inscriptions in Phoenician lettering. Political upheavals at Salamis are reflected in the issues of coinage which use first Cypriot lettering, then Phoenician, and then Cypriot alongside Greek.

Some interesting developments can be seen against the background of the struggle between Evagoras I, king of Salamis (411-373 BC), and the Persians. Evagoras, a representative of the Greek Teucrid dynasty, actively promoted Greek culture, and his coins have a notably fine artistic 'Greek' style. He also introduced Greek lettering for coin inscriptions and issued the first gold coins to be produced on the island [83]. Later, under another king of Salamis, Evagoras II (361-351 BC), a further innovation took place when Cyprus's first bronze coinage was minted, providing an alternative to the impractical small silver fractions used for the lowest denominations.

82 *Silver staters of the city-kingdoms: a) the ram with disc and crescent on a coin of Salamis (c.480 BC) are symbols of the worship of Aphrodite; b) a coin of Paphos, with a bull, winged disc and circular symbol of fertility, c.430 BC; c) a coin of Kition showing Herakles-Melqart with a club and bow, c.479-449 BC.*

83 *Gold fractions of Evagoras I of Salamis (411-373 BC): a) the head of Herakles-Melqart; b,c) the forepart and head of a goat; d) the Cypriot sign BA, signifying the royal title of the king.*

84 Above *The victory of Demetrios the Besieger off Salamis in 306 BC inspired the design of this silver tetradrachm. On the obverse Victory blows her trumpet on the prow of the war-galley; on the reverse Poseidon hurls his trident.*

85 Below *Cleopatra and her baby Caesarion, son of Julius Caesar, on a Cypriot bronze coin (44-30 BC). The Ptolemies of Egypt regularly struck coins for use within the island.*

When the Persian Empire was conquered by Alexander the Great (336-323 BC) Cyprus was first absorbed into Alexander's empire; then, after Alexander's death, the island was fought over in the wars between his successors – Ptolemy, and Antigonos the One-Eyed, with his son Demetrios the Besieger. One of the most interesting coinages of this period was issued by Demetrios after his victory over Ptolemy in a sea battle off Salamis in 306 BC [84]. The coins, some of which were minted at Salamis, depict Victory blowing a trumpet on the prow of a galley. Eventually, though, Ptolemy prevailed and Cyprus became a long-term possession of the Ptolemaic kings of Egypt.

The character of Cyprus's coinage was completely transformed by these dramatic historical developments. With the effective disappearance of the city-kingdoms the individuality seen in the earlier coinage issues was lost. From the time of Alexander the cities of Cyprus which still produced coins became merely branch mints issuing coins for local circulation as part of a monetary system controlled from outside. The city's identity was often reduced to a mere symbol or initial, subsidiary to the major coin type. Worth mentioning is a series of silver tetradrachms issued with the usual designs and in the name of Alexander the Great by Nikokles, the last king of Paphos in the 320s, on which the name of the local king is inscribed, secretively, in minute letters among the hairs of the lion scalp worn by Herakles.

Under the Ptolemies only four cities are identified as mints: Kition, Paphos, Salamis and Amathus. They produced issues in silver and occasionally also gold, which are virtually identical to the Egyptian series. They are distinguishable only by initials included within the design to identify the minting cities. These issues, which were mostly struck in the second century BC, can be dated precisely because the year of the reign is also included in the design, in Greek numerals prefixed by the letter L, a convention derived from Ptolemaic Egypt. Cyprus also produced issues of bronze coinage under the Ptolemies, though these cannot be attributed to individual mints. Some coins depicted the Cypriot goddess Aphrodite, others have designs simply copying the Ptolemaic bronze coins of Egypt.

Cyprus was ruled by the Ptolemies until 58 BC, when it became a Roman province, though for a brief period during Rome's civil wars the island was restored to the Ptolemies (47-30 BC). The coinage issued by Cleopatra VII in Cyprus at this time includes an interesting bronze coin depicting Cleopatra with her child, the son of Julius Caesar [85]. After the Battle of Actium and Cleopatra's death in 30 BC the island reverted to Rome.

The first coinage produced in Cyprus under Roman rule dates from the reign of Augustus (27 BC-AD 14). Until after Claudius' reign (AD 41-54) only bronze coins were minted on the island, and indeed this was usual for most eastern provinces of the Empire: production of silver coinage was confined to a few major centres, while numerous cities produced bronze 'Greek imperials'. Like most provincial coinages, the issues of Cyprus always portrayed a head of the emperor, or other member of the imperial family, on at least one side of the coin. The earliest Cypriot issues of the Roman period have inscriptions in Latin, but from the time of Claudius Greek was invariably used, as with most 'Greek imperial' coins.

Some of the early issues of the Roman province were signed by the governor; others have no inscriptions that clearly link them with Cyprus, but they can be identified as Cypriot either because of their reverse designs, depicting the sanctuary of Aphrodite at (Old) Paphos (see fig. 68) or the cult figure of Zeus of Salamis [86], or on the evidence of finds from the island. Under Claudius the first issues signed by the provincial council (Koinon) appear. Paphos, which was now the principal city in Cyprus, was the seat of the Koinon and it is presumed that most of the Koinon issues would have been minted there.

In the reign of Vespasian (AD 69-79) Cyprus was provided with a brief issue of silver coinage, together with related bronze coins, dated by the emperor's regnal years to the period 76-9. The bronze coinage was signed by the Koinon of Cyprus, but the silver was not, implying perhaps that it was issued directly by the Roman government, though the designs on the reverses refer again to the island's principal cults: Paphian Aphrodite and Zeus of Salamis. The bronze coins of Vespasian and his sons from AD 76 to 79, and also those issued in the name of the Koinon under Trajan (AD 98-117), have a style, fabric and metal which suggest they may have been minted at Rome, rather than in Cyprus. They contrast greatly with the earlier bronze coins which have a clearly local, not Roman, style.

Occasional issues only were produced after the reign of Trajan, and these were probably confined to bronze coins. An issue depicting Antoninus Pius (AD 138-61) and Marcus Aurelius Caesar has been attributed to Cyprus because most of the surviving examples have been found on the island. Further issues were produced under Septimius Severus (AD 193-211) and his family; these are now again signed by the Koinon. The last Cypriot coinage of the Roman period seems to have been issued under Severus Alexander (AD 222-35).

Finds from archaeological excavations indicate that Roman coins became increasingly common in Cyprus after the second century AD. It is likely that even before then the Roman denarius was the standard silver coin in use on the island, since only one issue of local silver coinage (under Vespasian) can certainly be attributed to Roman Cyprus. Other eastern silver issues, and bronzes, notably from nearby Antioch in Syria, also reached the island.

After the final cessation of local coin production early in the third century AD Cyprus relied entirely on imported coinage, even for its bronze pieces. In the course of that century the minting of local coinage came to an end throughout the Eastern Empire. A number of major provincial cities were now converted to production of Roman 'imperial' coinage as part of an empire-wide devolution of Roman coin production and issue, but Cyprus was left without a mint of its own. Thus all the coinage now going into circulation on the island had to be imported, and finds suggest that the mint of Antioch was by far the major supplier of currency to Cyprus in the late Roman Empire.

86 *The cult figure of Zeus of Salamis on a Cypriot bronze coin of the emperor Vespasian (AD 69-79), the reverse of fig. 13. He is shown with his eagle and is pouring a libation.*

Chapter Ten | Writing

FROM ABOUT 1500 BC at least some Cypriots could read and write. The earliest script used in Cyprus is known as Cypro-Minoan because of its affinities with the Linear A script of Minoan Crete. Like Linear A, Cypro-Minoan is assumed to be a syllabic script in which each sign represents a syllable, a combination of a consonant and a vowel, or a vowel alone. Similar too is the apparent left to right direction of the script. Neither Cypro-Minoan nor Linear A has yet been deciphered, which means that we do not know what languages they represent. Direct relations between Cyprus and Crete were minimal at the time when Cyprus adopted the script, but it could have been passed from Crete to Cyprus in Syria, with which both had close and lively commercial relations. Indeed, there may have been a Cypriot presence at Ugarit (see p. 40), which is the source of a tablet, inscribed in another version of Cypro-Minoan, with what seems to be a list of names of Semitic character; not really surprising, as Semitic was Ugarit's local language. Alternatively, both Cypro-Minoan and its successor, Cypro-Syllabic, may have a common (eastern) parent. Eastern influence on Cypriot literacy is certainly evident, since the Cypriot tablets are cushion-shaped and baked in a kiln in the eastern tradition. The tablets carry continuous texts in a different version of the script from that of briefer inscriptions which appear on clay 'balls' (of unknown use) and cylinders, pottery vessels and metal objects, as well as in designs on rings and sealstones.

It was not until the fourteenth century BC that the script became firmly established, continuing in use until the mid-twelfth century BC. Tablets with long texts have hitherto been found only at Enkomi [87] and at Ugarit on the Syrian coast. However, the discovery of items with brief inscriptions and bone *styli* (writing implements) at many of the other urban centres, including Kition, Hala Sultan Tekké, Kalavassos-Ayios Dhimitrios and (Old) Paphos, suggest that it was widely used. The different versions of the script perhaps represent different languages, but there is no evidence for the use of any other contemporary Aegean or Near Eastern, including Egyptian, languages in Late Bronze Age Cyprus, although a few imported objects have been found engraved with cuneiform inscriptions.

Many of the inscriptions from Iron Age Cyprus record dedications to deities or brief epitaphs for the dead, but there are a few documents referring to historical events or religious ceremonies. Inscriptions on coins name the issuing authority, initially the local kings of the cities (chapter 9). The principal script in Cyprus in the earlier Iron Age was

87 *About one quarter of a cushion-shaped clay tablet inscribed on both sides in the Cypro-Minoan script. The tablet was baked, in the Near Eastern tradition, and one column of the original text survives. The unequal length of the lines suggests that it may be a poem, but until the script has been deciphered the meaning of the texts remains obscure. From Enkomi, c.1200 BC. Width 9 cm (3.5 in).*

Cypro-Syllabic [88]. It has fifty to sixty signs, each denoting a syllable, and was usually written from right to left (perhaps reflecting Semitic influence), though a few inscriptions, including our first example (below), are written left to right. Cypro-Syllabic was used to write both Greek and Eteo-Cypriot. The latter remains an unknown language (the inscriptions are undeciphered) which cannot be related to any known linguistic family. It may therefore represent an indigenous Cypriot tongue still being spoken for most of the first millennium. The earliest evidence for the Greek language in Cyprus is a Cypro-Syllabic inscription on a bronze spit found in a tomb at (Old) Paphos with grave goods dated between 1050 and 950 BC. The script was not, however, in common use until the sixth century BC. It finally died out around 200 BC. Cypro-Syllabic is very probably related to Cypro-Minoan, and also has particular affinities with the Linear B script of Mycenaean Greece. This may be partly due to the fact that both are syllabic and were used to write Greek, albeit different dialects.

Cypro-Syllabic inscriptions form two principal series, the 'normal' (or 'common') and the Paphian. The 'normal syllabary' occurs from the north-west, in the area of Marion, to the east and from north to south. This version is also used for the Eteo-Cypriot inscriptions, most of which come from Amathus and the surrounding area. The Paphian syllabary was used in both (Old) and (New) Paphos and elsewhere in the south-west, with an extension northwards. The Greek dialect of even the earliest syllabic inscription is closest to that of Arcadia in the Peloponnese. This gives some credence to the different legends that credit Arcadian Greeks with the foundation of certain Cypriot cities.

It was a 'bilingual' inscription, with Phoenician and Cypro-Syllabic on the same stone [89], that assisted in the first decipherment of the Cypro-Syllabic script in the 1870s by the English Assyriologist George Smith. The earliest indisputable evidence for Phoenician in Cyprus is a tomb inscription of the ninth century BC, but it is not known where it was found. From about 800 BC Phoenician inscriptions are common at Kition, as one would expect; and with the spread of Phoenician influence within the island, particularly in the fifth and fourth centuries BC, the Phoenician script became more widely used. While the script survived only into the Hellenistic period, the language may have continued in use

88 *Marble statue base with a Greek inscription in the Greek and Cypro-Syllabic scripts which reads: 'Helloikos, the son of Poteisis, dedicated this as a vow to Demeter and Kore'. From the sanctuary of Demeter at Kourion (Curium), late 4th century BC. Length 28 cm (11 in).*

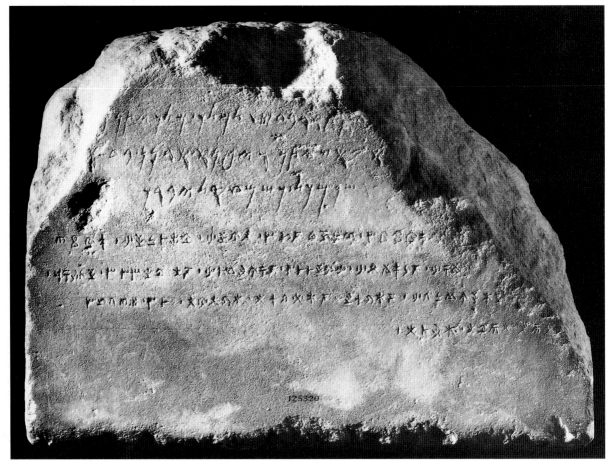

89 *Marble statuette base with a bilingual inscription in the Cypro-Syllabic and Phoenician scripts which records a dedication to Reshef-Mikal (in the Phoenician text) or Apollo Amyklos (in the Cypro-Syllabic Greek text), by the Phoenician prince Baalrom, son of Abdimilk in the fourth year of the reign of Milkyaton, King of Kition and Idalion. This inscription assisted in the first decipherment of the Cypro-Syllabic script in the 1870s. From the sanctuary of Apollo at Idalion, early 4th century BC (the precise dates of King Milkyaton's reign are not known). Width 40 cm (15.7 in).*

at Kition into the early Roman era. In Phoenicia itself the script had been standardised, so that it had an alphabet of twenty-two consonants by the ninth century. It was this standard form that the Phoenicians introduced to Cyprus and their western colonies. It was also adopted and greatly improved around 750 BC by the Greeks to write their own language. About the same time it reached Ita´y, where it was used for Etruscan and the Italic dialects. In Cyprus, of course, the language remained Phoenician.

Cuneiform, the wedge-shaped script of western Asia, is found occasionally in Iron Age Cyprus. The most famous document is a column erected by the Assyrian king Sargon II at Kition in about 707 BC, recording the submission of seven Cypriot kings. Other important documents in the cuneiform script mentioning the Cypriot kings and kingdoms have been found in the palaces of the Assyrian kings. The hieroglyphic (pictorial) script of Egypt was equally rare, but not unknown.

The Greek alphabet first appeared in Cyprus in the sixth century BC. It seems to have been officially introduced by Evagoras I at Salamis in the late fifth century; he put the Greek letter E together with the syllabary on his coins. However, it was not until a century later that the Greek alphabet became widely adopted, and about 300 BC Greek inscriptions begin to outnumber those in Cypro-Syllabic. Eteo-Cypriot survived until about 219 BC, but by the end of the century the Arcado-Cypriot dialect and with it the Cypriot-Syllabic script died out. Greek became the principal script and language of Hellenistic and Roman Cyprus [90], as it was in the rest of the eastern Mediterranean.

Although Greek was the official language of the Roman east, Latin, the language of the ruling power, was not completely unknown in Roman Cyprus. It occurs frequently on milestones of all periods, notably at the time of the construction of the road network in the first century AD and during the major reconstruction undertaken in the early third century. The few epitaphs of Roman soldiers, a single military inscription and dedications made by Roman citizens are all, not surprisingly, written in Latin. More unusual is the Latin in architectural inscriptions and under statues dedicated to emperors at Salamis, Soloi and Chytroi, all of the first century AD. It seems that certain civic authorities were trying to find favour with the ruling power in the early years of Roman domination.

90 *Gilded bronze pin with a Greek inscription on the shaft which reads: 'to the Paphian Aphrodite Eubola vowed this, the wife of Aratos the Kinsman [i.e. a member of the Ptolemaic court] and Tamisa'. The pin is crowned by pearl beads and the head below has four goats, separated by lotus flowers, springing from acanthus foliage with, above, four doves leaning forward to drink from the flower cup. The motifs illustrate some of the many traditions blended into the cult of the Paphian Aphrodite. From the sanctuary of Aphrodite at (Old) Paphos, 2nd century BC. Length 17.8 cm (7 in).*

Chapter Eleven | Weaponry and warfare

91 Right *A bronze weapon with a hooked tang. It is long enough to have been a sword and was made between 1900 and 1650 BC. Length 43.2 cm (17 in).*

AROUND 2500 BC the first metal weapons were made and used by the Cypriots. All are of eastern types, closest perhaps to those from southern Anatolia. There are signs of unrest in the seventeenth century BC, when the number of weapons buried in cemeteries increases enormously. Several occupation sites were fortified but these, with one exception (the fortress at Nitovikla in the south of the Karpass peninsula), are too far from the coast to have afforded protection from intruders arriving by sea. Both weapons and fortifications, therefore, are probably indications of internal strife.

The early weapon series, with hooked tangs for insertion into the handles or rivets by which they could be attached [91], ended in the mid-fifteenth century BC. Little is known about Cypriot weapons thereafter, until the late thirteenth and twelfth centuries BC. At that time cut-and-thrust swords [92] were introduced from Mycenaean Greece. The type is of European origin, probably brought to the Aegean world by barbarian mercenaries hired by the Mycenaean kings. A certain type of spearhead with a socket for the handle was also of Mycenaean Greek origin. Cypriot daggers and arrowheads of this period, however, owe little to the Bronze Age Greek world and any outside inspiration must have come from the Near East. Cypriot warriors in the twelfth century were equipped with armour of Mycenaean Greek type, including helmets, greaves and shields reinforced with metal bosses. Protection for the body was provided by scale corslets of Near Eastern origin which continued to be used until the end of the sixth century BC. If the motifs on pottery imported from Mycenaean Greece in the fourteenth and thirteenth centuries BC reflect Cypriot life, it can be assumed that warriors were transported to the battlefield in horse-drawn chariots. Herodotus, the Greek historian writing in the fifth century BC, tells us that war-chariots were still being used by the Salaminians in the battle against the invading Persian force in 498 BC.

Iron was used in Cyprus for knives, which were secured to their handles by bronze rivets, from the mid-twelfth century BC. In the following century iron became the principal material for swords and spearheads. Early iron swords are all versions of the older bronze cut-and-thrust variety. Alongside those of more modest dimensions were some impressive in their size and length. Modifications to the long sword were

92 *A copper and an iron sword of the 'cut-and-thrust' variety. The copper example (left) is one of a group of swords of an entirely Mediterranean type, originally of European origin and first wielded by barbarian mercenaries serving Aegean masters; from Enkomi, c.1150 BC. The iron sword (right) is the longest example of this particular type known at present. It was particularly popular in Crete, but ancestors of this weapon have also been found in Cyprus; from Amathus, c.7th century BC. Length of iron sword 51.5 cm (20.3 in).*

undertaken around 600 BC, but the persistent use of the type as late as the sixth century, shown by illustrations on vases as well as by actual finds, shows a distinct divergence from the weapons and tactics of contemporary Greece. Here a shorter sword had been introduced about 700 BC, at the time of the emergence of the hoplite phalanx, a formation of highly trained and well-equipped infantry. The retention of the long sword suggests that the Cypriots were rather less organised. Their armour and equipment, however, were improving: shields of perishable material were now reinforced with iron or bronze bosses, both rounded and spiked, and an all-metal spiked shield was used in the seventh century BC [93]. Subsequently modifications to these Cypriot types were made under the influence of the Greek hoplite shield. Shields with animal-head bosses were also used in Cyprus for much of the Archaic period. Originally Assyrian, this type perhaps reached Cyprus from Urartu (part of modern Turkey). It was certainly through, if not directly from, Cyprus that it became known in Crete.

Helmets in the earlier Iron Age were generally of Near Eastern varieties, but these were gradually modified under Greek influence during the later seventh and sixth centuries BC. Protective features including a nose-guard and cheekpieces [94], which project forward, were adopted from the Greek Corinthian type. From the late seventh century BC armour made of leather or linen with metal additions, such as neckguards and shoulder-flaps, began to replace the older scale body-armour. It seems likely that Cypriot warriors played a part in the development of the Greek 'composite corslet', made of a combination of metal and linen, which was worn from the second half of the sixth century. Other items of protective armour were of Greek

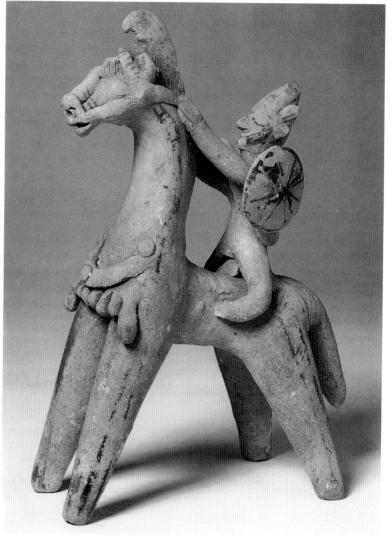

93 *Terracotta model of a warrior on horseback. The horse is protected by a tasselled breast-shield. The bridle has a tassle falling on to the nose and on the mane is a curving crest. The rider wears a helmet and carries a shield by a strap; 7th century BC. Height 16.5 cm (6.5 in).*

origin. A limestone sarcophagus of about 470/460 BC portrays Cypriot warriors with the armour and equipment of Greek hoplites [95]. They wear Corinthian helmets, the Greek composite corslet and greaves, and carry hoplite shields and long spears. There is also other evidence for the use of the hoplite shield in Cyprus at this time.

The Corinthian helmet was probably adopted, if not universally, towards the end of the sixth century BC. An example found in the Persian siege ramp of 498/7 BC at (Old) Paphos was apparently already a generation old when it was lost; this may have been worn by a Greek mercenary fighting on the Persian side, rather than by a Cypriot defender.

The Cypriot kings were much concerned with the fortification of their cities. As early as its foundation in the eleventh century BC Salamis had a mudbrick wall, but there is more information about the fortifications of many of the sites in the Archaic period. The walls were built of mudbrick on stone foundations. At Salamis they were now strengthened. At (Old) Paphos the wall had towers at intervals. The north-east gateway developed slowly; it started as the normal oriental type with twin bastions projecting at right angles from the city walls. The thoroughfare, 22 m (72.2 ft) long and 11.8-12.7 m (38.7-41.7 ft) wide, was restricted on the inside by a cross-bastion. Around 500 BC, shortly before the siege of the city by the Persians, the wall and gateway were considerably strengthened. The mudbrick faces were revetted with roughly squared limestone blocks and a developed sequence of ditch for-

94 Above Terracotta figurine of a three-bodied warrior. The helmets and shields are of Cypriot type but modified under Greek influence. The breastplates are among the earliest of an innovative type combining metal for the neckguard and arm guards with linen or leather, suggesting that the Cypriots played a part in the development of this new type of body armour. From Pyrga, late 7th century BC. Height 24 cm (9.6 in).

95 Limestone sarcophagus decorated in low relief with pairs of warriors hunting animals. The warriors are dressed and equipped as Greek hoplites. They wear Corinthian helmets and Greek 'composite' corslets (breastplates of metal and linen) and are armed with hoplite shields and long thrusting spears. The sarcophagus has feet, in the Cypriot tradition. Made in Cyprus, c.470-460 BC. From Golgoi. Length 239.4 cm (94.3 in).

tifications was provided. There was, therefore, a flat area between the wall and the ditch, which had steeply sloping sides. The gateway was narrowed by cross-bastions, so as to be less than 5 m (16.4 ft) wide (at the actual gate on the city side, it was only 2.9 m/9.5 ft). The cross-bastions were arranged so that the road went through a sharp double bend and could be covered by crossfire from soldiers on the parapets. The actual gate was closed by heavy wooden doors.

Excavations have revealed the story of the Persian siege of (Old) Paphos in 498/7 BC [96]. The Persians erected a huge ramp against the wall by the north-east gateway. The ramp was composed of rubble and broken limestone monuments from a nearby sanctuary. On this ramp they drove up their siege engines, which acted as battering rams and firing posts. Meanwhile, the Cypriots dug long tunnels and passages from inside the wall to come up within the ramp and under the gateway. In so doing they created huge cavities propped up with beams which were finally set on fire in order to topple the siege engines. Stone missiles may have been hurled from some kind of stone-throwing machine, perhaps an early catapult. Both sides fought with bows and arrows. Hundreds of arrow-heads and spearheads of bronze and iron were removed from the siege debris. Both eastern and Greek types are represented but it is impossible to know which were used by which side. It was also here that the Greek Corinthian helmet was found.

96 *View of the Persian siege of (Old) Paphos in 498 BC, after Sorrell. The Persians, whose camp is in the background, erected a huge ramp against the wall by the north-east gateway of the city. On this they drove up their siege engines, which acted as both battering rams and firing posts. The Cypriot defenders inside the city dug long tunnels and passages from inside the wall to come up within the ramp and under the gateway. Their aim was to topple the siege engines: the tunnels and passages had created huge cavities propped up by beams, which were then finally set on fire.*

Fortifications were still important to the Cypriot kings in the Classical period. At Idalion the citadel wall of the early fifth century BC was 10.5 m (34.4 ft) thick, with an inner core of small stones set in mud-mortar and faced with limestone blocks. A tower, perhaps part of a gateway, was built of fine limestone ashlars. This city withstood a siege by the Phoenicians of Kition and the Persians a generation before being captured by Kition in about the mid-fifth century BC. At (Old) Paphos the siege-damaged fortifications were put into a state of readiness again. The siege-ramp was surrounded by a revetment wall and included in the system. At Golgoi the fortifications of the fourth century, constructed of mudbrick on stone foundations, had houses built directly inside with their outer walls resting against the city wall, exactly as in the Greek city of Olynthus.

There is little information about the armour and weapons of Cyprus in the Hellenistic and Roman periods [97]. That they continued along Greek lines is suggested by the discovery of a fine helmet in a tomb of about the second century BC. This is of the so-called Thracian type with scalloped cheekpieces, apparently based on a type of cap worn by the Thracians from northern Greece. Paphos, the new town founded about 320 BC by Nikokles, the last king of the city-kingdom, was immediately fortified but only its rock-cut foundations survive. An impressive rock-cut ramp led up to the north-west gateway, one of the four gates of the city, which was flanked by two rectangular towers.

97 One of originally three panels of a mosaic floor in the south-eastern side of the central court of a Roman building (a patrician's house or public baths with palaestra) in the city of Curium (Kourion). The mosaic depicts different stages in gladiatorial combats. The central panel illustrated here shows the gladiators fully armed and ready to strike. They are named in Greek 'Margareites' and 'Hellenikos'. AD 250–300.

Underground chambers and passages cut into the rock close to the north gate may have housed units of the Ptolemaic garrison. The Hellenistic walls of Ayia Irini had houses built directly inside, like the fourth-century BC walls of Golgoi. The Ptolemies made little use of Cypriot manpower, although they had a fleet based in the island in their later years. The Cypriot population was swelled by the presence of a large mercenary force. The important towns all had their own garrisons. The commander-in-chief of all the forces was second in importance to the *strategos* (governor-general) and like him (and the majority of the company commanders) was a non-Cypriot. Many of the principal towns of Roman Cyprus, including Kition, Paphos, Curium, Lapithos, Soloi, Tamassos and perhaps Amathus, were fortified. Some use was made of Cypriot manpower in the professional Roman army: about two thousand were recruited at one time to serve overseas. The manufacture of a new type of arrow-head in Roman Cyprus suggests that they still fought with bows and arrows.

Although Cyprus was administered as a provincial backwater, the island's military history did not come to an end with Roman rule During the First Jewish Revolt of AD 115–17 Cypriot Jews rose against the Roman establishment, massacring thousands of the island's non-Jewish population, and reputedly destroying the city of Salamis. The large Jewish community in the island descended from colonists who may have arrived in the late fourth century BC. The rising was ruthlessly suppressed by Trajan's general Lusius Quietus, and Jews were forbidden in the island. In AD 269 Gothic tribes made a brief incursion, but despite these calamities the period of Roman rule in the island was relatively uneventful, and Cyprus was able to enjoy the benefits of stability under the *pax Romana*.

Postscript

For some nine thousand years Cyprus's position in the eastern Mediterranean, at a crossroads between the major civilisations of the ancient world, had opened the island to influences from many sources and had helped it to develop a unique and distinctive culture. Gradually Cyprus was assimilated into the Greek world and towards the end of this long period its own character became less distinct in the cultural sphere to which it now belonged.

The events of the fourth century AD, with the division of the Roman Empire in 395, mark the opening of a new period in Cyprus's history. During the century the island suffered drought, famine and earthquakes [98]; in AD 342 the city of Salamis was almost entirely destroyed. Rebuilt and renamed Constantia, it replaced the old capital at (New) Paphos as the seat of the governor, and again became the island's most important city. In AD 395 Cyprus was incorporated into the eastern Roman Empire, a period of transition which marks the end of this survey.

98 *An illustration of the dramatic consequences of the devastating earthquake which destroyed Curium (Kourion) in about AD 365. The skeleton of a mule is still attached to the trough to which it had been tethered in the courtyard of a house. The trough had been hurled into the wall, tilted and cracked, while the ground beneath had subsided.*

CHRONOLOGICAL TABLE

CYPRIOT HISTORICAL PERIODS	CYPRUS		MEDITERRANEAN
PROTO-NEOLITHIC	*Akrotiri* culture (*c.*8800 BC) First hunter-gatherers		
NEOLITHIC	*Khirokitia* culture (*c.*7000/6500-5700/5500 BC) Arrival of first settlers from Near East		
	Sotira culture (4600/4500-4000/3900 BC) First handmade pottery produced in Cyprus	4000	
CHALCOLITHIC (4000/3900-2500 BC)	*Erimi* culture Earliest metal objects in Cyprus	3000	Minoan civilisation of Crete (*c.* 3000-1100 BC)
TRANSITIONAL (2600/2500-2300 BC)	*Philia* culture ? Arrival of settlers from Anatolia		
BRONZE AGE Early (2300-1950 BC)		2000	
Middle (1950-1650 BC)			Hittite Empire of Anatolia (*c.*1750-1200 BC)
Late (1650-1050 BC)	Trading links firmly established with Egypt, the Near East and the Greek world		Mycenaean civilisation in mainland Greece (*c.*1600-1100 BC)
	Major wave of Greek immigration (*c.*1100 BC)		The 'Sea Peoples' active in eastern Mediterranean (late 13th & early 12th centuries BC)
IRON AGE Geometric (1050-750 BC)	'Dark Age' (1050-850 BC)	1000	
	Phoenician colony founded at Kition (mid-9th century)		Homer (*c.*750 BC)
Archaic (750-475 BC)	Heyday of city-kingdoms		
	Assyrian rule (*c.*707-612 BC)		
	Egyptian rule (*c.*570-526/5 BC)		
	Persian rule (526/5-333 BC)	500	Persian control of Ionia by *c.*540 BC
	Persian siege of Cypriot cities (498/7 BC)		Ionian Revolt (499-494 BC)
Classical (475-325 BC)	Struggle of Evagoras I of Salamis (411-374/3 BC) against Persian rule		Completion of Parthenon in Athens (432 BC)
	Submission of Cypriot cities to Alexander the Great (333 BC)		Alexander's victory over the Persians at Battle of Issus (333 BC)
Hellenistic (325-30 BC)	End of city-kingdoms		
	Annexation of Cyprus by Ptolemy I of Egypt (294 BC)		
	Cyprus becomes province of Rome (58 BC)		Sack of Corinth by Romans (146 BC) Greece becomes part of Roman Empire
	Cyprus in possession of Cleopatra VII (*c.*47-30 BC)		
Roman (30 BC-AD 395)	Cyprus reverts to Roman Empire (30 BC)	BC	
	Rising of Cypriot Jews (AD 116)	AD	First Jewish Revolt (AD 115-17)
			Byzantium (Constantinople) becomes capital of the Roman Empire (AD 330)
	Cyprus becomes part of eastern Roman Empire	395	Division of Roman Empire (AD 395)

Further reading

The Report of the Department of Antiquities of Cyprus, published annually, contains many articles on Cypriot archaeology, and 'Chronique des fouilles à Chypre', appearing annually in Bulletin de Correspondance Hellénique, provides a chronicle of current work in Cyprus. References to books and articles on specific topics will also be found in some of the books listed here.

Brown, A.C. and Catling, H.W., *Ancient Cyprus* (revised edn, Oxford, 1986)

Chypre au coeur des civilisations Méditerranéennes, Dossier d'Archéologie no. 205 (Paris, July-August 1995)

Cook, B.F. (ed.), *Cypriote Art in the British Museum* (London, 1979)

Hill, Sir George, *A History of Cyprus*, vol. 1 (Cambridge, 1940)

Hunt, Sir David (ed.), *Footprints in Cyprus* (1982, revised edn, London, 1990, reprinted 1994)

Karageorghis, V., *Cyprus from the Stone Age to the Romans* (London, 1982)

Karageorghis, V. (ed.), *Archaeology in Cyprus 1960-1985* (Nicosia, 1985)

Maier, F.G., *Cypern: Insel am Kreuzweg der Geschichte* (2nd edn, Munich, 1982)

Maier, F.G. and Karageorghis, V., *Paphos: History and Archaeology* (Nicosia, 1984)

Morris, Desmond, *The Art of Ancient Cyprus* (Oxford, 1985)

Peltenburg, Edgar (ed.), *Early Society in Cyprus* (Edinburgh, 1989)

Reyes, A., *Archaic Cyprus* (Oxford, 1994)

Tatton-Brown, V. (ed.), *Cyprus BC: 7,000 Years of History* (London, 1979)

Tatton-Brown, V. (ed.), *Cyprus and the East Mediterranean in the Iron Age* (Proceedings of the Seventh British Museum Classical Colloquium, London, 1989)

Acknowledgements

My first debt is again to Mr and Mrs Constantine Leventis and the Leventis family for their support in every aspect of this project. I am grateful too to Mr B.F. Cook, the former Keeper of Greek and Roman Antiquities in the British Museum, and Dr D.J.R. Williams, the present Keeper, for their encouragement. The draft text of the first edition was read by Mr B.F. Cook, Professor F.G. Maier and Dr Susan Woodford, and for this second edition I am particularly indebted to Dr R.S. Merrillees and again to Professor F.G. Maier, and to Ms J. Lesley Fitton, Professor O. Masson and Professor E. Peltenburg. I would like to thank them all for their help. Dr Ian Carradice has kindly updated his chapter on the coins. For advice on specific points I am most grateful to Miss Carol Andrews, Dr D.M. Bailey, Professor Sir John Boardman, Dr Diana Buitron, Dr Lucilla Burn, Professor J.N. Coldstream, Dr P.T. Craddock, Dr Elizabeth Goring, Miss Hero Granger-Taylor, Dr M. Henig, Dr Maria Iakovou, Dr I.D. Jenkins, Dr Ellen Macnamara, Dr G. Markoe, Mr T. Mitchell, Dr A. Reyes, Dr R. Senff, Dr D. Soren, Dr Judith Swaddling, Dr S. Swiny, Mr C. Walker, Dr Susan Walker and Dr D.J.R. Williams. The Directors, both past and present, and all the staff of the Department of Antiquities of Cyprus have given their full co-operation. Many of my colleagues have helped in the production of this book. I am indebted to them all, among them Mr R. Flint, Mr B. Jackson and Mr J. Lloyd who helped with the ordering of photographs and access to literature, and especially to Mrs Marian Vian who typed the original text, Miss Susan Bird for the maps, Enkomi plan and siege drawing and our photographers, initially Miss Jane Beamish, Mr P. Gardner and Mr P. E. Nicholls, and for this new edition again Mr P. E. Nicholls and Mr S. Dodd of the British Museum Photographic Service. I would also like to thank British Museum Press, in particular the editors, Miss Jenny Chattington for the first edition and Ms Nina Shandloff for this new edition, and also Miss Celia Clear, the former head, and Mrs Emma Way, the present head, of the Press. Finally I must thank my children Hugh, Miranda, Lucy and Robert, and my husband, Tim.

Veronica Tatton-Brown

July 1996

The author and publishers are grateful to the following for permission to reproduce illustrations not supplied by the British Museum Photographic Service: Department of Antiquities of Cyprus (4, 14, 18, 19, 22, 25, 34), Xenophon Michael (8, 32, 60, 69, 73, 87), Sonia Halliday Photographs (21, 23, 24), T.W.T. Tatton-Brown (78, 97), Ekdotike Athenon (15), After the plan of the Mission Archéologique Française d'Alasia (Prof. C.F.A. Schaeffer and Dr J. Courtois) and of the Director of the Department of Antiquities of Cyprus (Dr P. Dikaios), reproduced by permission of Verlag Philipp von Zabern (16), Photo École Française d'Athènes/Ph. Collet (17), Vassos Karageorghis (20), M.L. Katzev (33), Lemba Archaeological Project (46), Metropolitan Museum of Art, New York (Cesnola Collection, purchased by subscription 1874-6) (95) and David Soren (98). Figures 1 and 76 are the author's own.

Museum registration and catalogue numbers

Numbers are given in the order in which objects are described in the captions. GR, G&R: Department of Greek & Roman Antiquities; *BM Cat.*, *BMC*: *British Museum Catalogue*; CM: Department of Coins & Medals; WAA: Department of Western Asiatic Antiquities.

Cover *BM Cat. Terracottas* A 45
2 *BM Cat. Jewellery* 194, 102
3 *BM Cat. G&R Glass* 14
5 *BM Cat. Terracottas* A 188, A 182, A 225
6 *BM Cat. Vases* C 134
7 GR 1929.2-11.2
8 Cyprus Museum, Nicosia, 1934/11-2/2
9 *BM Cat. Vases* C 732
10 GR 1897.4-1.300
11 GR 1873.3-20.339
12 *BM Cat. Sculpture* C 352
13 *BMC Cyprus* 22
17 Limassol Museum AM 805 (83.2.1)
26 GR 1979.12-14.1
27 GR 1920.12-20.1
28 GR 1872.8-16.98
29 *BM Cat. Bronzes* 111, 107, 112
30 GR 1903.12-15.48
31 GR 1876.9-9.112
32 Cyprus Museum, Nicosia, Canadian excavations no. A 13
34 a) *BM Cat. Vases* C 71; b) GR 1939.2-17.71; c) *BM Cat. Vases* C 64
35 a) GR 1884.12-10.69; b) GR 1981.12-18.53
36 a) GR 1985.10-8.1; b) *BM Cat. Vases* C 252
37 GR 1897.4-1.999
38 GR 1897.4-1.996
39 GR 1911.4-28.1
40 GR 1927.12-13.2
41 *BM Cat. Vases* C 885, C 1025
42 *BM Cat. Vases* C 974
43 *BM Cat. Vases* C 904
44 a) *BM Cat. G&R Glass* 364; b) *BM Cat. Vases* C 940; c) GR 1881.8-24.70; d) *BM Cat. Lamps* Q 500; e) GR 1881.8-24.50
45 a) *BM Cat. Lamps* Q 2453; b) GR 1908.4-11.10; c) GR 1896.2-1.298; d) GR 1872.7-26.6; e) GR 1876.9-9.40; f) GR 1884.12-10.258; g) GR 1888.11-12.1; h) *BM Cat. Lamps* Q 2580; i) GR 1876.9-9.47
46 Cyprus Museum, Nicosia, LL 54
47 On loan from the Old Palace School, Croydon
48 *BM Cat. Vases* C 303, C 311, C 261, C 302
49 *BM Cat. Terracottas* A 16, A 15
50 *BM Cat. Vases* C 838
51 *BM Cat. Sculpture* C 12
52 GR 1910.6-20.1
53 GR 1873.3-20.87
54 *BM Cat. Sculpture* C 154
55 *BM Cat. Sculpture* C 131
56 *BM Cat. Sculpture* C 321
57 *BM Cat. Terracottas* A 406, A 410
58 *BM Cat. Sculpture* 1992
59 a) *BM Cat. Jewellery* 779-80; b) *Jewellery* 299-300; c) GR 1897.4-1.208, 209; d) *Jewellery* 623; e) *Jewellery* 580
60 Cyprus Museum, Nicosia, Palaepaphos, Evreti tomb 8
61 *BM Cat. Jewellery* 1646-7
62 *BM Cat. Finger Rings* a) 1641; b) 175; c) 1242; d) 851
63 *BM Cat. Jewellery* a) 2407-8; b) 2526-7; c) 2723
64 *BM Cat. Jewellery* 552, 550
65 *BM Cat. Gems* 527, 481
66 *BM Cat. Jewellery* 2053, 1728-9, 1958
67 GR 1929.10-14.1
68 *BMC Cyprus* 62
69 Cyprus Museum, Nicosia, Enkomi, 1963 French excavations no. 16.15
70 *BM Cat. Terracottas* A 123
71 *BM Cat. Terracottas* A 151, A 152
72 *BM Cat. Sculpture* C 216
73 Kourion Museum, Episkopi, Kourion T 1775
74 a) *BM Cat. Terracottas* A 84; b) *BM Cat. Sculpture* C 30; c) *Sculpture* C 242
75 *BM Cat. Sculpture* C 164
77 *BM Cat. Sculpture* C 429
79 *BM Cat. Sculpture* C 431
80 *BM Cat. Paintings* 8
81 GR 1871.17-1.1
82 a) *BMC Salamis* 23; b) *BMC Paphos* 39; c) *BMC Citium* 6
83 a) *BMC Salamis* 51; b) *Salamis* 53; c) *Salamis* 54; d) CM 1920.3-26.9
84 CM 1873.8-3.1, R. Payne Knight Bequest
85 *BMC Cleopatra* 2
86 *BMC Cyprus* 22
87 Cyprus Museum, Nicosia, Enkomi, 1953 excavations of the Cyprus Department of Antiquities no. 1687
88 *BM Cat. Greek Inscriptions* 968a
89 WAA 125.320
90 *BM Cat. Jewellery* 1999
91 GR 1969.12-31.100
92 *BM Cat. Bronzes* 72; GR 1894.11-1.689
93 GR 1876.9-9.91
94 GR 1866.1-1.298 and 299
95 Metropolitan Museum of Art, New York, 74.51.2451

Index

Index